More Praise for *The Social Labs*

"A profoundly important and timely b
—Joseph Jaworski, author of the inte

"An innovative, powerful new approach for lasting social change."
—**Minh-Thu Pham, Director of Public Policy, United Nations Foundation**

"An important milestone in learning how to address our most profound challenges."
—**Adam Kahane, author of *Solving Tough Problems*, *Power and Love*, and *Transformative Scenario Planning***

"Prototyping and systemic approaches have worked for entrepreneurs— Zaid Hassan shows us how they can work for complex social issues."
—**Howard Rheingold, author of the bestsellers *Virtual Reality*, *The Virtual Community*, *Smart Mobs*, and *Net Smart***

"Anyone interested in doing something about the complex, multi-cultural, economico-politico-social problems that the planet is facing must read this book."
—**Edgar H. Schein Professor Emeritus, MIT Sloan School of Management, and author of *Humble Inquiry***

"Opens up the space to see, seed, and grow better possibilities."
—**Dr. Angela Wilkinson, Counselor for Strategic Foresight, Organisation for Economic Co-operation and Development**

"A highly readable, provocative narrative filled with insights, questions, and, above all, a deep yearning to know how best to make a difference."
—**Margaret J. Wheatley, author of *Leadership and the New Science* and, most recently, *So Far from Home***

"A brilliant book, brave and honest."
—**Mustafa Suleyman, cofounder and Chief Product Officer, DeepMind Technologies**

"A powerful and practical book—read it."
—**Tim Harford, author of *The Undercover Economist Strikes Back* and Senior Columnist, *Financial Times***

"Truly personal, analytical, and luminous...essential reading for all those who aspire to effect deep and sustainable social change."
—**Gabriella Etmektsoglou, Director, New York University Berlin**

"Offers a promising approach to achieving real change."
 —**Wael Hmaidan, Director, Climate Action Network International**

"An extremely compelling and readable manifesto for people looking for effective solutions beyond packaged development programs."
 —**Melissa Finn, Lecturer, Department of Political Science, Wilfrid Laurier University**

"Shows how to engage with complexity and offers a compelling alternative to plans that can be outdated by the time they are written."
 —**Danny Burns, Team Leader, Institute of Development Studies, University of Sussex**

"Required reading for policymakers, practitioners, academics, and engaged citizens everywhere."
 —**Milla McLachlan, Director, Southern Africa Food Lab**

"Hassan is a facilitative leader of systemic change. Read this book if you seek wisdom and practical experience."
 —**Hal Hamilton, Codirector, Sustainable Food Lab**

"This is the type of book I will always have two copies of: one as an immediately useful narrative, and one to share with others."
 —**George Roter, CEO and cofounder, Engineers without Borders Canada**

"Innovative, informative, accessible, and relevant. Strongly recommended."
 —**Wajahat Ali, cohost of Al Jazeera America's @AJAMStream**

"A must-read for all who are trying to tackle the many social problems afflicting our planet."
 —**Kamran Bokhari, Vice President, Middle Eastern and South Asian Affairs, Stratfor, and coauthor of *Political Islam in the Age of Democratization***

"Zaid Hassan understands processes of social change."
 —**Dr. H. A. Hellyer, Nonresident Fellow, Foreign Policy, The Brookings Institution**

"This book will help you not just find better answers to systemic problems but build better strategies for changing the systems themselves."
 —**Alex Steffen, Planetary Futurist in Residence, IDEO, and author of *Carbon Zero***

THE SOCIAL LABS REVOLUTION

THE SOCIAL LABS REVOLUTION

A NEW APPROACH TO SOLVING OUR MOST COMPLEX CHALLENGES

Zaid Hassan

A Reos Publication

BK

Berrett–Koehler Publishers, Inc.
San Francisco
a BK Currents book

Berrett-Koehler Publishers, Inc.
235 Montgomery Street, Suite 650
San Francisco, CA 94104-2916
Tel: (415) 288-0260; Fax: (415) 362-2512; www.bkconnection.com

Ordering Information

Quantity sales. Special discounts are available on quantity purchases by corporations, associations, and others. For details, contact the "Special Sales Department" at the Berrett-Koehler address above.

Individual sales. Berrett-Koehler publications are available through most bookstores. They can also be ordered directly from Berrett-Koehler: Tel: (800) 929-2929; Fax: (802) 864-7626; www.bkconnection.com.

Orders for college textbook/course adoption use. Please contact Berrett-Koehler: Tel: (800) 929-2929; Fax: (802) 864-7626.

Orders by U.S. trade bookstores and wholesalers. Please contact Ingram Publisher Services: Tel: (800) 509-4887; Fax: (800) 838-1149; E-mail: customer .service@ingrampublisherservices.com; or visit www.ingrampublisherservices .com/Ordering for details about electronic ordering.

Berrett-Koehler and the BK logo are registered trademarks of Berrett-Koehler Publishers, Inc.

Printed in the United States of America

Berrett-Koehler books are printed on long-lasting acid-free paper. When it is available, we choose paper that has been manufactured by environmentally responsible processes. These may include using trees grown in sustainable forests, incorporating recycled paper, minimizing chlorine in bleaching, or recycling the energy produced at the paper mill.

Library of Congress Cataloging-in-Publication Data
Hassan, Zaid.
  The social labs revolution : a new approach to solving our most complex challenges / Zaid Hassan. — First edition.
      pages cm
  Includes bibliographical references and index.
  ISBN 978-1-62656-073-4 (pbk.)
  1. Social problems—Research—Methodology. 2. Problem solving. I. Title.
HN29.H35 2014
361.1—dc23   2013041859

FIRST EDITION

19 18 17 16 15 14 || 10 9 8 7 6 5 4 3 2 1

Produced by BookMatters; edited by Tanya Grove, proofread by Janet Reed Blake, and indexed by Leonard Rosenbaum. Cover designer: Kirk DouPonce, DogEared Design.

For Mia

Corruptio optimi quae est pessima.

CONTENTS

FOREWORD
by Joi Ito, Director, MIT Media Lab

The Media Lab, the interdisciplinary research center I direct at the Massachusetts Institute of Technology, faces a challenge: how do we connect the discoveries we make in our labs with the real problems people face in their communities?

I found myself confronting this problem when I organized a group of students, faculty, and advisors to visit Detroit, the city where I grew up, to explore how the Media Lab might help address the many challenges the city faces. Community organizer Shaka Senghor quickly set me straight. Hundreds of people come to Detroit hoping to solve the city's problems. The only way these solutions work is when they're developed in partnership with the people actually affected by these problems. The Media Lab can be a powerful contributor to addressing the problems Detroit faces, but only in partnership with citizens, organizations in the community, and local government.

Zaid's book offers practical insight into how to make such partnerships work. This book offers a new approach to the complex, real-world problems facing communities, organizations, cities, nations, and the world as a whole—just the sorts of problems we enjoying tackling at the Media Lab. Social laboratories bring together civil society, industry, government, and the people directly affected by the challenges in question to seek creative new solutions from a cooperative and interdisciplinary perspective. This approach to problem solving—bringing together the best thinking from different disciplines, approaching a problem from different perspectives—is precisely the approach that leading research labs in the hard sciences are taking to address the thorniest problems in their fields.

One of the challenges research labs have is moving from thought to action. My experience with technology start-up companies has taught me that prototyping and iterating is how agile companies succeed. Zaid has taken these and other ideas that have found traction in Silicon Valley and applied them to complex social problems.

Zaid builds on his decade of experience to offer a book that is an effective, practical, and exciting guide to implementing a visionary new approach to social challenges. Whether you are trying to transform a dysfunctional school in your neighborhood or help a nation escape a cycle of famine, you will find powerful new ideas, approaches, and methods in this book that will inspire and transform your work.

PREFACE
Notes from a Practicing Heart

We will see
That day. . .
When the cruel mountains of injustice
will blow away like cotton-wool. . .
We will see

— from *Hum Dekhenge,* by Faiz Ahmed Faiz

Since 1942 my family has fled from our home four times, leapfrogging from India across continents, twice within my own lifetime. On three occasions we witnessed civil war, communal violence, and mass murder. Each time, we've had to rebuild our lives, having left virtually everything behind. The fourth move came as tanks were rolling into Kuwait not far from where we lived, in the first Gulf War.

My childhood memories begin in 1970s South London. They include my uncle coming home out of breath and covered in blood after being attacked by skinheads on his way back from work. He moved back to Karachi soon after that, where he has been living happily since. In 1980 we moved peacefully from London to New Delhi, after a year in Bombay. My parents had decided that we needed to widen our horizons beyond Margaret Thatcher's Britain.

A few years after we moved to New Delhi, the Indian prime minister, Indira Gandhi, was assassinated by her Sikh bodyguards. Widespread communal riots followed. I remember looking out of a car window toward a burning house, set on fire by rioters. In my mind, I can still see the slow movement of the curtains on fire and the shimmering flames pouring out of the window. Seeing black scorch marks on the New Delhi pavement, I remember asking what they were and my shock at the answer. Roving mobs had targeted members of the Sikh community, dragged people on to the streets, and set fire to them. I remember my parents making the decision to leave India with the words, "This place hasn't changed."

We moved to the United Arab Emirates, where we spent several largely uneventful years. Then Saddam Hussein invaded Kuwait, launching the first Gulf War. I remember craning my neck out of my bedroom window in the middle of the night to watch US military convoys pass by, sometimes taking hours to pass. I remember playing Ping-Pong with GIs on shore leave, most of them only a few years older than me. I remember tuning into US Armed Forces Radio after everyone had gone to bed and listening to bands singing US college hits.

There are numerous stories, told over the years by my grandmother and great uncles and aunts of the Partition of India, leading to the creation of Pakistan, when a million people died. Our community was split across the subcontinent and beyond. Then from my parents and uncles and aunts came the stories of the civil war that led to the creation of Bangladesh. I remember feeling an underlying frisson of adrenalin in talking about such bloodshed and the experience of surviving, of being here and not there.

My entire life I've reflected on the universal nature of conflict and loss, and why such events transpire. I've pondered the sequences of events that bring them about and asked what we can do to ensure they don't happen again.

In seeking the answer to these questions I've been driven, sometimes reluctantly, to take on many different roles. Throughout my time as a student, an apprentice, a dot-com entrepreneur, an activist, a writer, a facilitator, a consultant, a process designer, and a strategist, I've reflected on the experiences I've been blessed with and on my own practice with a view to understanding and preventing violent conflict. I've written down these lessons. Each phase of my journey has contributed, in unexpected ways, to a practice focused on effectively addressing complex social challenges. This book represents a summing up of what I have learned so far.

My aim in writing this book is to address the question of what it takes to tackle our most profound social, environmental, and political challenges in practice.

My experiences and reflections over the years have led me to conclude that violent conflict is a largely avoidable product of ineffective approaches to complex social issues. Dominant efforts to address our most serious challenges waste precious resources, time, and talent. These planning-based approaches—so common across government, civil society, and even business—represent a neo-Soviet paradigm, one that is spectacularly out of step with what we now know about complexity, about systems, about networks, and about how change happens. Another approach is needed.

This book has four core goals:

1. To make *the case* that the planning-based approach of addressing complex social challenges leads to certain widespread social collapse.

2. To describe *the principles* of social labs—a new, more effective prototyping-based approach for addressing complex social challenges.

3. To describe *the practice* of social labs through an account of two "first generation" social labs, demonstrating their effectiveness.

4. To outline *a practical theory of systemic action* that can be used to design next-generation social labs.

In 2004 I started working for Generon Consulting, a small, highly innovative Boston-based organization. Generon's unofficial, courageous, and insane mission was to address "ten global problems in ten years." The means to achieving this mission was the Change Lab, a prototype social lab that Generon developed working with others in the Boston/MIT/Society for Organizational Learning (SoL) community. The following years were spent conceiving, convening, designing, and running social labs around the world. Some of these succeeded wildly; others failed painfully.

During this time I read hundreds of books on social change and group processes in an effort to grasp the foundations of the approach we were undertaking. I produced a number of documents and a few articles. I also wrote hundreds and hundreds of pages of journal entries filling a couple of shelves of black Moleskine notebooks.

In early 2007, I helped cofound a successor organization to Generon called Reos Partners. *Reos* is derived from the Greek word *rheos* meaning *flow*, the opposite of *stuck*. Since then, we have continued to develop the work started with Generon. Designed to be international from the outset, Reos currently has offices in eight cities around the world. In addition to consulting work, Reos focuses on capacity building and launching new labs.

In this decade we have convened many thousands of stakeholders, including CEOs of global corporations, young executives, ministers, civil servants, civic leaders, and grassroots activists. We have worked on all continents on issues as diverse as global food systems, climate change, child protection, public health care, community development, and making financial systems more sustainable.

The materials I have drawn on to write this book come from work conducted by my colleagues at Generon Consulting, Reos Partners, and the wider community that we are a part of.

While I see our work as being on the cutting edge, I'm also deeply conscious of the bleeding edge, a place where my colleagues and I struggle with gaps in our practice. This bleeding-edge practice is explored later in this book through the idea of next-generation laboratories.

The approach taken to write this book is formally known as an inductive approach to research, resulting in what is known as *grounded theory*.[1] The principle behind inductive approaches is that *in the particular lies the universal*, which means examining specific experiences and drawing general conclusions from them. The theory of action outlined in this book is directly built on my experiences running multiple "first generation" social labs.

This book aspires to tell a story, the story of our greatest challenges and how we might address them. This story unfolds in three parts.

The first part concerns the unique nature of the challenges we as humanity are facing. Chapters 1 and 2 explore why these challenges are different from those of the past and why planning-based responses to complex challenges fail.

The second part outlines the struggle to come up with a better response. Chapters 3 and 4 show two social labs—the Sustainable

Food Lab, focused on the global food system, and the Bhavishya Lab, focused on child malnutrition in India. Chapter 5 discusses the results of first-generation social labs, outlines a new framework for understanding these results, and begins articulating the broader implications of these experiences.

The third part of this story goes further in sketching out the general implications of the social-labs approach. Chapter 6 explains why this approach is effective at addressing complex social challenges and introduces the rise of a new type of practitioner, the *agilista*. Chapter 7 outlines steps toward a theory of systemic action built on a decade of prototyping social labs. Chapter 8 shows how to start social labs in seven steps. Finally, the conclusion outlines a number of next-generation social laboratories and offers a broad vision of how some of our most serious challenges might be solved.

INTRODUCTION
What Are Social Laboratories?

The power of solutions lies primarily in the people who believe in
and own them.

— V. Srinavas

Current approaches to addressing complex social challenges are
not working. There is much to celebrate: the number of people
involved in change initiatives, the increasing amounts of money
being invested in those initiatives, the steadily declining costs of
technology and the attention being given to social innovation. The
underlying problems however, from species loss to public debt,
continue to grow.

Social fabrics are increasingly strained under loads they were
never intended to contain. Inequality is growing. Direct action
has either become a strident call for someone else to take action
or the frantic alleviation of symptoms that leave underlying causes
largely intact. There's increasing pressure on individuals to change
their behavior around environmental issues and to take on the
burden of austerity measures or cuts in basic services. The sociologist Ulrich Beck describes this situation as an attempt to find
"individual solutions to systemic contradictions."[1]

Throw an ashtray in any direction, and you'll hit a messy, complex challenge. It's difficult to escape the persistent feeling that while our problems are already big and bad, they're in fact getting bigger and badder. It's harder and harder to believe people who tell us that things are actually getting better. The future is changing in our lifetimes from a magical place to a place best avoided, a dark place that's becoming difficult to contemplate.

Into this situation comes a very simple premise. We have scientific and technical labs for solving our most difficult scientific and technical challenges. We need social labs to solve our most pressing social challenges. Thomas Homer-Dixon explains:

> The public not only needs to understand the importance of experimentation within the public service; it needs to engage in experimentation itself. To the extent that the public explores the solution landscape through its own innovations and safe-fail experiments, it will see constant experimentation as a legitimate and even essential part of living in our new world. To the extent that the public understands the importance of—and itself engages in—experimentation, it will be safer for all of you in the public service to encourage experimentation in your organizations.[2]

Social labs have been quietly brewing for almost twenty years. Hundreds of people around the world have been and are developing social labs. Thousands more have participated in them. There are labs focused on eliminating poverty, on water sustainability, on transforming media, on government, on climate, on social innovation, and on many more issues. A growing number of people are focusing their heads, hearts, and hands on addressing complex social challenges.

The people running these labs represent a new breed—they're not simply scientists or academics, and neither are they activists or entrepreneurs. They're all of these things and a few things we don't have good names for yet. They're making the case for and launching social labs around the world, trying to address some of our most difficult challenges.

Social labs are platforms for addressing complex social challenges that have three core characteristics.

1. *They are social.* Social labs start by bringing together diverse participants to work in a team that acts collectively. They are ideally drawn from different sectors of society, such as government, civil society, and the business community. The participation of diverse stakeholders *beyond* consultation, as opposed to teams of experts or technocrats, represents the *social* nature of social labs.

2. *They are experimental.* Social labs are not one-off experiences. They're ongoing and sustained efforts. The team doing the work takes an iterative approach to the challenges it wants to address, prototyping interventions and managing a portfolio of promising solutions. This reflects the *experimental* nature of social labs, as opposed to the project-based nature of many social interventions.

3. *They are systemic.* The ideas and initiatives developing in social labs, released as prototypes, aspire to be *systemic* in nature. This means trying to come up with solutions that go beyond dealing with a part of the whole or symptoms and address the root cause of why things are not working in the first place.

These characteristics are not arbitrary. Nor are they convenient. Getting really diverse groups of people to simply step into a room together is hard, let alone trying to get them to act together. Taking an experimental approach requires not only discipline but also a degree of stability and commitment rare in a project-obsessed world. Addressing the root causes of challenges eschews easy and popular political wins in favor of longer time frames and greater uncertainty.

While none of these characteristics is convenient, each is necessary, deeply so. Each characteristic represents hard-won conclusions wrestled at great cost from many thousands upon thousands of hours of trial and error. Each represents countless workshops where many stakeholders shared their most agonizing and difficult challenges. And perhaps more than anything else, together they represent integrity and honesty—they are not what we want solutions to look like, but what we have found they actually look like when effective.

There are, of course, aspiring social labs that do not meet these characteristics any better than programmatic or project-based responses. My contention is that social labs or any intervention aiming to address social challenges that do not have these three characteristics "baked in" will be ineffective or fail.[3] The reasons for this are the nature of complex social challenges, explored in Chapters 1 and 2.

The Sustainable Food Lab was the first social lab I was involved in that embodied these three criteria. Its focus was how to make the global food system more sustainable. The global nature of the challenge meant that participants came from around the world, as well as from different sectors.

The Food Lab initially brought together approximately thirty participants, drawn from corporate food companies, such as Unilever and General Mills; civil society organizations, such as World Wildlife Fund and The Nature Conservancy; and government officials, including representatives from Brazil and the Netherlands.

These participants formed the lab team, who committed to

physically working together for approximately twenty days over two years. They were supported by a secretariat, of which I was a part. The role of the secretariat was to design, facilitate, document, and organize the overall lab, building what could be thought of as its *container*. Over two years, we met together five times: in the Netherlands, Brazil, the United States, Austria, and Costa Rica. Since then, the team has grown and met many times in many other countries.

The lab team started working together by gaining firsthand experience of the system we were trying to change. They traveled as a group to different parts of the food system, such as food distribution centers, big companies, supermarkets, and small and larger farms in several countries. We reflected together on what they had learned. From this reflection came a broad portfolio of initiatives, which were tested and implemented in a process called prototyping. These initiatives ranged from working with small farms in the Global South to trying to shift procurement practices in large corporations, mostly headquartered in the Global North.

WHAT DOES IT MEAN TO BE WINNING?

How successful has the Sustainable Food Lab been?

Director of the Center for Organizational Learning at MIT Peter Senge said, "The Sustainable Food Lab is the largest and most promising systemic change initiative I know of."[4]

The first formal meeting of the lab took place in 2004. What has happened since then? Today sustainability is well entrenched on the radar of global food companies. The Sustainable Food Lab has played a key role in making this happen, having grown to become a platform for innovation in the global food system. From an initial group of twenty-two institutions, today it has almost seventy members.

One business leader reflected on its value, "I am convinced that the world is not capable of feeding nine billion people in the second half of this century, in our grandchildren's world. . . . We see the system cannot work. What the Sustainable Food Lab is doing has never been done before, this intersection of private and public institutions. This is the greatest hope I have for finding a way through these complex dynamics to a livable world."[5]

So has the Sustainable Food Lab solved the original problem it set out to address? One of its missions was to move sustainability practices from niche to mainstream. This shift has clearly been achieved—the global food system is more sustainable today than when the lab was conceived and launched, and it can claim no small credit for this.

Many more decision makers are aware of the challenges they face and many more organizations are engaged in actively addressing these challenges. Prior to the lab it was clear that lots of individuals in the mainstream food system were concerned about broader sustainability issues, but most were not. Corporate attitudes were either defensive or, at best, focused on minimal compliance, as opposed to seeing sustainability as a competitive advantage or as being part of their broader civic role.[6] A key example of this shift is Unilever's sustainability policies, which were heavily influenced by their long-standing participation in the lab. In 2012 Unilever announced, "it would endeavor to decouple growth from its environmental impact. By 2020, Unilever aims to halve the environmental footprint of its products and to improve the lives of a substantial number of smallholder farmers."[7]

The Food Lab, and other social labs, generate at minimum four sets of outputs: *physical capital* (new services or infrastructure), human capital (new capacities and skills), *social capital* (increased trust and collaboration), and finally, *intellectual capital* (new knowledge and learning). As we will see in the cases that follow, these outputs contribute directly to preventing the collapse of key systems.

The success of any lab—scientific, technical, or social—must be measured through multiple indicators, as opposed to relying on a binary logic of did it work or not. Particularly when concerned with either basic science or long-term challenges, such as cures for cancer, for example, progress is sometimes hard to measure in the short term. It may be premature to ask a medical technician, "How many people have you cured this quarter?" But just because the answer to this question might be "none," this does not indicate progress is not being made. Over time, however, progress is much easier to see, and results can be more clearly articulated.

The contrast between how we approach scientific and technical challenges and how we treat social challenges is stark. Whereas the natural sciences have moved on from a Newtonian worldview, it sometimes feels in the social spheres that we are still trapped in mechanical, linear ways of thinking. Instead of supporting talented and committed teams to seek permanent solutions to our most serious challenges as we do in the sciences or in the technology sector, we fund tightly controlled five-year plans. This leaves little space for learning, innovation, and change.

Teams that create real and lasting change on the ground are rarely invested in or funded. When it comes to social challenges, plans are what get funded. The teams responsible for both the formulation and implementation of plans come as afterthoughts, if at all. The nature of plans requires that we predict the future, telling funders and sponsors in advance what we will produce every quarter, sometimes for years on end.

Imagine a company like Google, at inception, being asked to package its work into a five-year plan. Imagine an investor telling Larry Page that he has to tell them what inputs he needs every quarter and what outputs he will produce every quarter. And if there is a difference between his predictions and reality, his funding will be at risk. And while he's at it, overheads must be kept below 20 percent. Further imagine that the investor doesn't really care about where the talent will come from. Clearly such a scenario is absurd. Google is famous for its anti-planning stance.[8] Yet imposing this neo-Soviet model is the norm when it comes to addressing complex social challenges. We have to ask ourselves not only what does it mean to be *winning* or *losing* in the social sphere but what does it actually mean to play?

PLAYING IN THE WORLD CUP

> Nothing in this world is difficult, but thinking makes it seem so. Where there is true will, there is always a way.
>
> — Wu Cheng'en

Everywhere I go, I meet people who want to change things. They want to change the education system or address issues such as climate change or eliminate extreme poverty. Sometimes these people are young, and sometimes they are experienced. Sometimes these people are activists or entrepreneurs; sometimes they are government employees or elected officials; sometimes they work in business as chief executives or corporate responsibility professionals. Sometimes they are resource rich, and sometimes they are not.

The first thing that usually strikes me about these encounters is the nobility of the intention. People really care fiercely about each other. By and large they want to help each other and do something about the suffering, unfairness, or injustice in the situations we are all confronted with. More and more people are taking up the hard work of changing such situations. A belief that we can change things is spreading. I feel hopeful.

The second thing that strikes me is the lack of realism that all too often accompanies such intentions and desires. I often hear from people who do not seem to entirely grasp the nature of the challenges they seek to address. Many people are working as individuals, even as they work within massive institutions, on problems that affect many thousands, or even millions, of people. Then when I talk to well-intentioned and resource-rich organizations, they do not seem to be very effective. Reports recommending action seem to be drowning out action. It's as if we believe that writing a report is 90 percent of the work. Finally, I feel there is too much contentment with whatever is being done, regardless of impact. I start feeling less hopeful.

People approach my colleagues and me to help them with problems that are on par with winning the World Cup: eliminating child malnutrition, addressing climate change, or making the global financial system more sustainable, and so on.

A typical conversation goes something like this:

Person: I want to house the homeless (or address poverty or any one of a dozen honorable intentions. . .)

Me: That's great. How do you want to do that?

Person: Well, I'm very passionate about it, but I'm not sure. . .

Me: Ok, well to start, what kind of resources are investing in this venture?

Person: I plan on working on it one day a week and would like your help running a two-day workshop.

You might think this is a crazy conversation, but it happens in various forms all the time, albeit usually couched in slightly more sophisticated language. And I struggle. How do I respectfully break the news that an individual working one day a week is highly unlikely to address poverty in Africa? For starters, you need a team. Would someone think it was possible to train for the World Cup only one day a week?

What about those institutions that have overcome the challenges of time and resources? What about all the multibillion-dollar initiatives with hundreds of employees? What about a resource-rich organization like the World Bank with its mission "Working for a World Free of Poverty"? What about governments?

Well, as anyone who has watched any competition knows, there are winners and losers. And the correlation between wealth and winning is not always clear cut. All too often we believe that the solution is simply a matter of money or resources. This isn't true for sports and it isn't true for complex social issues.

Brazil, to take one example, has won the World Cup five times, while simultaneously having a low GDP and being one of the most unequal societies in the world. Michael Lewis, in his bestselling book, *Moneyball*, tells the story of the Oakland Athletics, where he explores the question, "How did one of the poorest teams in baseball, the Oakland Athletics, win so many games?"[9] There are also countless examples of teams spending millions of dollars and getting nowhere. As Michael Lewis points out, "It still matters less how much money you have than how well you spend it." Money is certainly a factor, but the challenge clearly goes beyond material resources.

The most important question about winning the World Cup, or achieving any big goal, is to ask how badly do I want this? And critically, how badly do *we* want this? If we don't want it badly enough, if we're unsure, then it's highly unlikely we will be willing to go through the pain, make the sacrifices, and build the skills required to win a World Cup. Everything flows from this commitment to play.

I remember seeing a documentary about Usain Bolt, the fastest man in the world. At one point during training, he staggered off the track and spent a few minutes throwing up. He scowled up at the camera and said, "I hate training." Hubert Dreyfus, a sociologist who has studied how we acquire skills, comments, "To become competent you must feel bad."[10]

THE SCALE-FREE LABORATORY

I don't want to scale things up, I want to get them right.
— Derek Miller, *The Policy Lab*

All this talk of World Cups implies that social labs can be applied only to big challenges, like the sustainability of the global food system. Interestingly, scale is one of the issues that most preoccupies actors working in the social realm. The usual assumption is that we start small and then grow big. Common questions, particularly in donor communities, include "How will your initiative scale up?" and "What is your scaling strategy?" These concerns are, however, largely irrelevant.

Just as a game of football can be played almost anywhere with very little equipment or can be played with professional teams in vast stadiums, social labs can be run at any scale. This could range from a school or an organization to a community, a city, a country, a region, or the world. A good example of this comes from South Africa.

In mid-2007, my colleagues Marianne Knuth and Mille Bojer helped launch a South African initiative called Kago Ya Bana (KYB), which means "Building Together for Our Children." The work was located in Midvaal Municipality, located midway between Johannesburg and Pretoria with a population of just under one hundred thousand people. It focused on the challenges faced by children and families suffering from HIV and AIDS. KYB represents a successful lab undertaken at community level.

One of the participants reflected on what she had learned working on KYB: "Since KYB, I feel hopeful because every stakeholder is taking responsibility and there is shared ownership of the problem. Every part of the child feels represented—from nutrition, to access documentation and involving parents. We are tackling the problem at all levels and it feels like, wow, we are a village raising a child."[11]

The decision of scale is, in many ways, the first decision that needs to be made about what sort of social lab to run. People who want to play football have a decision to make: are they going to play informally and kick a ball around with their friends, play in a local league, or strive to play professionally? The same decision needs to be made around a lab. What level of challenge are we up for? And there is no wrong answer.

Instead of seeing social interventions as always needing to take scaling up into account, the social realm is scale-free by nature.[12] A social lab can be designed to operate at any scale, depending on the intentions of the people in it. It will grow in whatever direction and way is needed and doesn't necessarily require central planning.

There is one caveat in creating purely local labs. When we start examining purely local challenges, we discover that the source of our problems lies far outside the boundaries of our communities—be that the death of manufacturing or adverse environmental effects brought about by climate change. In other words, while a social lab can be run at any scale, we soon discover that we're not cleanly separate from the big, bad world.

If successful, a social lab will produce direct results addressing the challenge at the scale it's designed for, be that a community or a country. Labs can also, however, produce results *beyond* the scale they're designed to work in. This happens when inspiring innovation and disciplined use of the intellectual capital—inevitable parts of a lab—build capacity in people who go on to do other things.

Once we're clear that we really do want to try to win a World Cup (or eradicate unemployment in our community, or address climate change, etc.), we're faced with the question of how best to proceed, of how to play. It's not simply that we lack resources, time, or people willing to tackle our most complex social challenges. Rather, we lack a theory of action; we need some way of guiding our actions, a practical theory. How do we deploy our talents, our time, our money, and our resources as a society? Where do we find the will to tackle complex challenges?

The practice of social labs aspires to answer these questions. This practice offers anyone interested in addressing complex social challenges an option. In contrast to this option, however, is the dominant planning-based response. It's into this dominant response that most attention, energy, and resources go. If we understand complex social challenges better, then we'll see that such investments are nothing short of disastrous—hence the dire need for a different approach.

A CASCADE OF SOCIAL LABS

> The prize for solving the problems we now face will be to have more interesting problems to solve in the future.
> — Alex Steffan

A social lab is not, of course, a silver bullet that solves our most complex social problems. Social labs represent a new direction, different from business-as-usual (BAU) responses. They represent a pragmatic attempt to act in the face of increasingly complex situations in a way that increases the odds of addressing situations systemically at their roots.

Perhaps one of the most exciting developments in the last few years is the birth of many new social labs. While each on its own is exciting enough, an ecology of labs together promises a revolution in how we address complex social challenges. Some of these labs are what could be thought of as social labs, while others represent a democratization of scientific and technological labs. The possibilities generated by these labs working together are endless. Given enough social labs, we will see vibrant ecologies sprouting up to support them. The wonder of it is that this is what's actually happening.

There has been an explosion in the number of labs focused on addressing complex social challenges. SociaLab, based in Chile, focuses on new enterprises to alleviate poverty. Some of these labs, such as the Abdul Latif Jameel Poverty Action Lab (J-PAL) at MIT, are formally labs in the sense of being housed in a university and staffed by academic practitioners.[13] Others are not formally known as labs, but, for all intents and purposes, are because of their practices. For instance, my friend Bob Stilger has helped create Resilient Japan, which is focused on community responses to the 2011 earthquake and tsunami.[14]

Labs are also springing up as a way for organizations to learn with their partners, such as Greenpeace's Mobilisation Lab, or MobLab, which is "designed to capitalize on Greenpeace's fearless embrace of the experimental . . . [and] provides the global organization and its allies a dynamic, forward-looking space to envision, test, and roll out creative new means of inspiring larger networks of leaders and people around the world to break through and win on threats to people and the planet."

At Reos, my colleagues and I have been busy with several labs, including ones on climate change, community resilience, and state collapse.

With support from us, the Rocky Mountain Institute runs the eLab, which is "a state-of-the-art forum to accelerate the transformation of the U.S. electricity system."[15] Another example is the Open Contracting Initiative. Along with the World Bank and numerous other stakeholders we are working toward transparency in government contracting.[16]

In addition to social labs, there has been an exponential increase in a number of *maker* or *fab* labs. These labs deploy technologies such as 3-D printing in order to democratize the manufacture of just about anything imaginable. A movement springing from MIT's Centre of Bits and Atoms, Fab Labs, has open-sourced its technology, and now we are seeing labs popping up from Afghanistan to California.[17] The potential of social labs increases when coupled with this new generation of tech labs.

Considering the development of an entire ecology of social labs and having uncovered the theoretical and practical gaps in first-generation social labs leads us to an exciting question: what would we have if we built on first-generation social labs, theoretically and practically, making the improvements we know we need to make? We would have a battle-tested, mature approach. We would have a theory of systemic action to help guide us in addressing complex social challenges. We would have a revolution in how we address humanity's most pressing challenges.

1

The Perfect Storm
of Complexity

When you want to know how things really work, study them
when they're coming apart.

— William Gibson, *Zero History*

For every complex problem there is an answer that is clear,
simple, and wrong.

— H. L. Mencken

Humanity has always suffered plagues, famines, floods, and warfare. In modern times we have faced new horrors, such as nuclear
weapons and AIDS. One common stance toward our current
challenges is that we will adapt just as we have always adapted.
The trouble with this stance is that our current challenges are profoundly different from those of the past. Our familiar modern
responses no longer work because they're based on a fundamental
misunderstanding of what we are facing.

THE PERFECT CHALLENGE

Just how different our challenges are crystallized for me in the summer of 2008. It began with a mysterious call from two strangers. I met them in an empty cafe on Cowley Road in Oxford, not far from where I live. Both had been working in Yemen for a number of years. They wanted to know if we could help. I knew very little about Yemen and so asked them to explain the situation to me. The pair, Henry Thompson and Ginny Hill, spoke in hushed voices, occasionally looking around to make sure no one else was listening. I was bemused at their behavior and not quite sure what to make of them.

Yemen, they told me, was in serious trouble. It was collapsing. The facts were startling. Bordering Saudi Arabia and Oman, on the other side of the Red Sea from Somalia, Yemen occupied a geostrategic location due to the Suez Canal and its proximity to the oil fields of Saudi Arabia and the United Arab Emirates. One of the oldest civilizations in the Middle East, it also had the youngest and fastest growing population in the region, over twenty-three million people, 50 percent of whom were under fifteen.[1]

First, Al Quaeda was using Yemen as a major base for operations. Second, the country was suffering from two incipient civil wars, which threatened to flare up at any moment. One was a secessionist movement in the south, and the other involved a religious minority in the north. In addition, Yemenis were running out of what meager resources they had: water, oil, food, and foreign exchange to buy food. Yet, Yemen had four times as many AK47s as people.[2]

Finally, they explained, the crux of the problem was that a cabal of criminals and quasi-criminals ran the country, a situation sometimes known as state-capture. This *shadow elite* lived behind anti-missile walls and in some cases held no official positions despite wielding great influence. When I asked about official channels, they looked at each other and shrugged. Could we help?

WHAT IS A COMPLEX SOCIAL CHALLENGE?

The situation in Yemen is a textbook example of a complex social challenge because of three characteristics: (1) the situation is *emergent*, (2), as a result, there is a constant flow of *information* to negotiate, and (3) this means actors are constantly *adapting* their behavior.[3]

Complex social challenges are *emergent* because their properties arise from the interaction of many parts. Imagine the difference between throwing a rock and throwing a live bird. The rock will follow a path that is *predictable,* that is, it can be predicted with a high degree of accuracy in advance. The path of the bird, on the other hand, is *emergent,* which means that path cannot be predicted in advance. It emerges from the interactions of many factors from the physiology of the bird to environmental factors. The *system* of the person (throwing the bird) and the bird is therefore said to be characterized by emergence.

In complex systems new *information* is constantly being generated.[4] When we study a complex system, we are deluged by new information. If we tied a GPS to the bird and tracked its movements, we would be capturing a new stream of information about where the bird was going. (According to Nate Silver, "IBM estimates we are generating 2.5 quintillion bytes of data per day, more than 90 percent of which was created in the last two years."[5])

This new information gives rise to the third characteristic of a complex system, that of *adaptive* behavior. This means that actors in complex systems are constantly and autonomously adjusting their behaviors in response to new information. This feedback loop in turn gives rise to a whole new set of emergent characteristics. If our task is to re-capture the bird once it's been thrown, then we use information to adapt our behaviors to ensure we succeed.

These three characteristics make complex challenges distinct by nature from technical challenges. Ronald Heifitz and his colleagues at Harvard's Kennedy School of Government define a challenge as being technical when the problem and the solution are clearly defined.[6] And they point out that confusing adaptive, or complex, challenges with technical challenges is a classic error.

An example of a technical challenge is sending a man to the moon. The problem is clearly defined and the solution unequivocal. Implementation may require solving many difficult problems, but the desired outcome is plainly understood and agreed upon. In contrast, multiple perceptions of both the problem and the solution are characteristic of complex systems.

Complex challenges are therefore dynamic and can change in unexpected ways over time, whereas technical challenges are relatively stable and static in comparison. The nature of gravity, for example, is not changing while we try to come up with solutions for putting a man on the moon. This is just one reason why it is hard to address complex social challenges.

In the past, everything was less connected. Today, interconnectivity is rapidly increasing, creating an age defined by its complexity. This connectivity has many dividends, but it also means that our landscape of challenges has changed dramatically in the last few decades. In the past, problems could be dealt with in isolation, while today, most of our most intractable social challenges are deeply interconnected. They don't respect man-made boundaries, such as national borders. The nature of interconnectivity means that we are seeing challenges that are entirely new *and* fast changing.

These challenges are sometimes referred to as *wicked problems*, a phrase coined in the early 1970s.[7] The trouble with the word *wicked* is that it makes us think that complex situations are somehow deviations from a *non*-wicked norm, that they are somehow temporary aberrations. And the problem, if you like, with the word *problem* is that it conveys the impression that everyone thinks of the situation as a problem (when some actors, typically those holding minority positions, might not).

One practitioner compares christening complex challenges as wicked to a story of a grandfather and the coming of cars.[8] The grandfather couldn't understand why cars didn't behave like horses (resulting in many accidents) and considered them wicked. Much as we might love our grandfathers, calling complex social challenges *wicked* betrays a way of thinking that doesn't make much sense today. Forty years ago we had just started to wrap our heads around the idea of complexity. Since then we have learned a lot, and many ideas from complexity science are in common use. Complexity is the norm for us—not an anomaly—and there is no returning to a simpler "non-wicked" time.

THE FUTILE OPTIMISM OF OPTIMIZATION

> It's 1959. The USSR is on the brink of Utopia. Comrades, let's optimize!
>
> — Francis Spufford, *Red Plenty*

Today it is common to address a wide range of complex social challenges using methods that are technical and planning based. Together they define a culturally dominant technocratic approach, which characterizes efforts at addressing challenges as diverse as public health care, environmental degradation, poverty, and inequality.

This dominant technocratic approach was born during the early twentieth century, a time when the belief that science would solve all human problems was widespread. The work of mathematicians such as Kurt Gödel and physicists such as Werner Heisenberg shattered this belief. By then, however, the technocratic paradigm had rooted itself deeply in an entire generation of problem solvers, who then passed it on.

Technocratic approaches typically seek to optimize, that is, to incrementally improve a situation through efficiency gains. For example, if ten thousand people are hungry, then a technocratic approach would seek to ensure that every day some of these people were fed, thus incrementally improving the situation. The end goal, of course, is to ensure that all ten thousand people are fed. This is a classic optimization strategy.

Optimization makes sense in some instances, such as when the number of hungry people is static and not increasing. Economists call this *inelastic* demand, as opposed to *elastic* demand.[9] This means that if we manage to feed two hundred hungry people per day, in fifty days we would have fed all ten thousand people, therefore optimizing our way toward solving the problem of ten thousand hungry people.

This strategy is dramatically less effective in dynamic situations. Imagine that we feed ten thousand hungry people at a rate of two hundred per day. If, for whatever reason, the number of hungry people increases by 5 percent per day (compounded), then we're in trouble. After five days of feeding two hundred people a day, we end up with just under 11,300 hungry people. After 10 days we end up with just over 13,300 hungry people, after 50 days we wind up with nearly 70,000, and so on. The dream of optimization, of course, is the other way round—that we increase the number of hungry people we feed every day by a percentage, which, when compounded over years, leads to a utopian society free of hunger.[10] Of course, all of this assumes that gains will not be wiped out by unexpected events, such as a famine or some other natural disaster.

Another problem with technocratic approaches, including optimization, is that it addresses parts in isolation, rather than the whole. This could look like feeding a small number of hungry people by cutting down massive swathes of rainforest, which helps a small minority, while vast resources are spent with massive long-term negative impact. A side effect of optimization is that the underlying causal dynamics are frequently untouched.

This is what's happening in Yemen with malnutrition. The system is generating more malnourished people every day than can be fed. Efforts to support them are helping small parts and are being outstripped by the dynamic nature of the challenge, where the problem as a whole is getting worse day by day.

The same logic applies to many issues, including climate change, deforestation, and poverty. Imagine that ten new light bulbs are turned on every second, each emitting a tiny puff of carbon dioxide. This pumps greenhouse gases into the atmosphere, which increases the risk of dangerous climate change.

An optimization response would be to turn off three light bulbs every second, striving in time to turn off four or five, and believe this is adequate. Unfortunately this leaves us with a net increase of emissions, despite our efforts. That is what's happening with greenhouse gases dramatically increasing the probability of dangerous climate change.

All complex challenges have what could be thought of as an engine that produces the symptoms we are most concerned about, be that too many hungry people or too many greenhouse gas emissions. We see these symptoms as trends. For example, one of the trends governing the situation in Yemen is population growth, which, in itself, is not a problem. But when coupled with other trends, such as steadily declining agricultural productivity, we can see how it creates the complex social challenge of malnutrition.

This reflects a situation where demand for different forms of capital is increasing, including natural capital, such as fossil fuels and food. Simultaneously, there is a decline in our ability to meet this increasing demand sustainably. This is represented, for example, by declining forests, topsoil loss, less fresh water, and the shrinking envelope of carbon dioxide we can safely emit—which puts limits on how much fossil fuel we can safely burn. In other words, we are now hitting boundaries beyond which our actions seem to be causing irreparable damage to critical ecosystems.

It's not simply that we're running out of resources. The story is more complex. Ramez Naam demonstrates how we have used technological innovation to produce greater output from the same natural resources. For example, we have managed to dramatically increase yields from the same acre of land and convert greater percentages of solar energy into electricity. While the efficiencies are getting better and costs are dropping, they are not dropping fast enough to shift the underlying negative trends. Furthermore, market-based approaches have yet to figure out what to do with the environmental consequences of economic growth.[11]

Technocratic approaches, therefore, represent a bet, a "grand wager" that our ability to optimize will be faster than the rate at which our problems grow.[12] If our problems are growing exponentially and our ability to optimize is growing linearly (or worse, declining), then we are staring at a mathematical certainty of collapse. This is what happened with the Soviet Union and what's currently happening with many responses to complex social challenges across the world.

YEMEN AS A NATURAL EXPERIMENT

My first response to the request for helping in Yemen was "No, of course we can't help." The situation was too far along in its trajectory of collapse. Henry and Ginny wanted to bring the elite—including the shadow elite—into a room and run a scenario planning exercise on the future of Yemen.[13] The elite would then see the implications of what they were doing to the country, and this insight would cause them to act proactively in the interests of the whole.

I pointed out that the shadow elite would not voluntarily step forward into such a conversation. Our usual approaches would not work with people who were loath to step up in any formal way, which is what defines a shadow elite.

Originally I assumed this situation was unique to Yemen. However, I later came across the work of Janine Wedel, a professor and author, who argues that the phenomenon of the shadow elite is widespread: "A new breed of players has arisen in the past several decades . . . whose manoeuvrings are beyond the traditional mechanisms of accountability. They, for example, play multiple, overlapping, and not fully disclosed roles."[14] And what she describes applies to Yemen as well as many other places, including the United States, Europe, and China.[15]

Even if by some miracle the shadow elite did agree to participate, I was dubious that such a top-down exercise would result in fundamental change. I offered advice relating to the nature of the problem but largely felt that I didn't have anything useful to say. My two guests politely thanked me and left.

A few months later they invited me to a talk called "Crisis in Yemen: A Holistic Approach?" being given by a state department official, who had worked at the US Embassy in Yemen for many years. Out of curiosity, I put on a suit and tie and caught the train to London.

The talk was at the Royal Institute of International Affairs, known as Chatham House. Ginny worked there, helping organize a forum on Yemen. Officially a think tank, Chatham House serves as a global rallying point for those concerned with foreign affairs issues. This constellation, including both Yemenis and non-Yemenis, was out in full force that day.

As the talk ended, I turned to my neighbor and asked, "I might have missed something, but what's the holistic approach?" He looked at me a little blankly and said, "Oh, he doesn't really have a holistic solution, he's just saying that we need one."

Later, I quizzed organizers on the purpose of the talk. One person told me that the speaker was there to deliver a message to friends of Yemen. The startling message was that there was time to act in order to avert disaster in Yemen, but if this window was passed, the response would unfortunately shift to the Pentagon and the military planners.

Soon afterward I read a *New York Times* article with the headline "Is Yemen the Next Afghanistan?" which made me both intensely concerned and curious. In it Robert Worth writes, "I spoke to a number of American officials in Washington and to a variety of diplomats at the embassy in Sana. They all told me the same thing: no one has a real strategy for Yemen."[16]

Over the next few years I went to Chatham House whenever there was a talk on Yemen.

My colleagues and I had worked on many challenges singularly: food and energy security, child malnutrition, water stress, and security issues. Almost all of these were happening in Yemen simultaneously, creating the perfect storm of complex challenges.

Yemen is what Jared Diamond calls a "natural experiment."[17] These are situations we could not recreate for reasons both practical and ethical. We are unable to cause a drought in order to study the effects of water instability on communities; nor would we do so in good conscience. Naturally occurring phenomena present us with options to study situations and learn from them.

Yemenis were facing down all the problems that other countries, regions, cities, and people were conceivably going to face in the future. A lot could be learned from examining not just the trajectory of challenges in Yemen but also the responses to these challenges. Yemen represents the future of a lot of places.

While the circumstances are unfortunate, Yemen is at the forefront of developing innovative strategies for how to address complex challenges. It is a little like the Dutch experience of building dikes. With the challenges of climate change, the Dutch are working all over the world helping communities build dikes to protect themselves from the rising oceans. It's conceivable that the Yemenis will build a skill set to address a complex series of interlinked problems before anyone else.

The Yemen Forum gatherings I attended were consultations with civil society on what should be done. They were also often attended by Yemeni government representatives. But it seemed that few people had any faith in the ability of Yemen's government to do anything.

At the end of a Chatham House event I chaired, I conducted an impromptu straw poll, asking the audience to raise their hands if they had faith in the government's ability to come up with a centralized response to Yemen's problems (as opposed to a decentralized one).[18] The only people who voted in the affirmative were a handful of Yemen government officials sitting in the front row. To my astonishment, all other hands stayed down. I was astonished because these were the same people who told me that plan A for Yemen ran straight through its government.

When I asked one foreign office official (FCO) why they haven't tried to catalyze a track-two effort, involving NGOs and other civil society actors as well as government, he gave me the official line: they had to deal directly with the government of Yemen because doing anything else would be seen as interference in the sovereignty of a nation. This was not even vaguely true in practice. When I asked the same question to the head of a UN agency struggling with a myriad of problems in Yemen, he responded, "Plan A has to be to work with the government; perhaps if that fails, we will examine a plan B."

TOO BIG TO FAIL, TOO BIG TO JAIL

What seemed both obvious and crazy to me about Yemen was that everyone seemed to be saying that plan A had not only failed but had been failing for years. The unfortunate narrative in the international community was that the government of then President Saleh had little capacity to implement anything; it did not keep its promises and could not be trusted.

Every couple of years the government of Yemen would come up with a new plan and present a "Christmas list" of requests to the international community—asking for the plan to be funded. Each time this happened, the international community would demand assurances that the plan would be implemented, and of course very little actually happened.

The government representatives from Yemen who came to these meetings were repeatedly lectured on their failings by their Western counterparts. They sat with their arms crossed, listening mostly in silence, occasionally responding to questions or to say that they needed more resources and support. I asked one deputy minister how he managed to sit silently while being repeatedly patronized like that. He gave me a wry smile and shrugged.

I felt there was little cognizance in the international community of the nature of the challenges being faced by the Yemenis. From my work globally, I knew that it wasn't as if someone else had figured out how to deal with these issues effectively, resource rich or not. It wasn't simply that the Yemenis were doing a bad job, as was implied—they were also faced with a titanic set of challenges that no one anywhere really knew how to address.

Yemen was too big to fail. This idea, first popularized during the US 2008 financial crisis, applies to countries and development programs as well.[19] In these situations, a system, be it a government or a program, is deemed as too politically sensitive to fail. So it is kept alive at massive cost, despite the fact that it may be failing in almost all dimensions beyond the political.

The situation in Yemen was fascinating because there was such widespread agreement about the failure of the Saleh regime, but the international community seemed to think it was powerless to do anything. Saleh was not simply too big to fail—he was too big to *jail*.[20] Indeed, during the Arab Spring, it was the Yemenis who forced Saleh to resign, but he managed to negotiate an immunity deal in which he would not be held accountable for anything that happened during his tenure.

What was I seeing? What were the stakeholders who came to Chatham House hoping would happen? What were they doing? It felt like people were operating on autopilot—they were all doing their jobs, and, almost regardless of what was *actually* happening, they would keep doing them. They were going through the motions of business as usual, or BAU.

2

The Strategic Vacuum

We are losing the skills of cooperation needed to make a complex
society work.

— Richard Sennett, *Together: The Rituals, Pleasures
and Politics of Cooperation*

Social labs as a new approach to solving complex social challenges
compete with existing business-as-usual (BAU) approaches. The
relative efficiency of one strategy over another can be evaluated
only by considering the nature and cost of BAU approaches as a
response to our challenges.

BUSINESS AS USUAL

Randy Shilts, a journalist who documented the spread of AIDS
in the United States provides a sobering example of business as
usual.[1] During the early years of the AIDS epidemic, the blood
bank industry in the United States found doctors who questioned
the evidence that AIDS resulted from a virus that could be trans-
mitted through blood. These doctors argued in public that screening was not needed. Screening blood would mean the introduc-

tion of expensive processes and a crisis of confidence in the entire system of blood banks, which would in turn mean that the blood banks would lose a lot of money.

The decision not to screen blood resulted in many unnecessary deaths through contaminated blood. The lack of scientific consensus on the nature of AIDS allowed the blood banks to operate in BAU modes, even as the gay community and activists generated political pressure by pointing out that dying people required a response.

Shilts writes

> Years later, when it was clear that hundreds were dying because the blood industry and federal regulators at the FDA heeded the calls from people like Joseph Bove, the doctor would pull a copy of his speech from his shelf at Yale to show that his 1983 presentation at NYU was, technically, accurate. "I wrote 'evidence is minimal,'" said Bove. "I was extremely cautious about my choice of words. I didn't want to go on the record either way. I was smart enough not to say it wasn't there. Technically, I was not inaccurate."[2]

BAU is what we do normally. It's what we're most used to doing and consists of those activities that we're most comfortable doing. When a new challenge arises, BAU means taking an approach in which we're operating from deep within our comfort zone. It means not having to experience the discomfort of something that's new, with all the vulnerabilities that brings. It means not taking risks with our professional reputations. And in the words of one lab team member, "If you always do what you've always done, then you'll get what you always got."[3]

Business as usual is the dominant response in the face of complex challenges. Four spheres—the developmental, humanitarian, security, and battle—define BAU today.

The Developmental Sphere

Developmental responses attempt to cover basic needs for people, to ensure that they have an adequate supply of food and water, that they have shelter, and that they have a degree of safety in responding to injury and illness (such as in the Shilts example above). Education is usually seen as a high-leverage way of addressing these issues.

The developmental sphere is difficult to clearly define because the activities that shape it come from a combination of government, business, and civil society entities. The primary actor in this sphere, however, is government.

In domestic contexts, developmental responses are covered by social services and associated ministries, such as the US Department of Health and Human Services or the National Health Service in the UK. In so-called developing-world contexts, where government is seen as unable to meet basic needs, international aid seeks to plug the gaps, either by supporting governments or through provision of direct services.

In the developmental sphere businesses actively provide food, and in some cases shelter and health care, but are typically not seen as decision makers because this sphere is considered, in theory (but not in practice), to be independent of market forces. People are not provided for by their governments and cannot afford services at market rates and therefore rely on the developmental sphere.

The organization of the developmental space as the primary domain of governments is profoundly neo-Soviet in structure, practices, and culture. With the fiscal crisis, this neo-Soviet character has been strengthened through what is being called the results-based agenda.[4] The idea is to pay for results.

Unfortunately one consequence of this seemingly simple idea is increased gaming of the system, where actors are forced to compromise (e.g., by fabricating data) because in practice what is being asked of them might not be possible. Studies have shown that while such results-based approaches can deliver progress in the short term, in the long term they risk collapse. Two academics from Oxford studying the National Health Service in the UK recently remarked:

> In the 2000s, governments in the UK, particularly in England, developed a system of governance of public services that combined targets with an element of terror. This has obvious parallels with the Soviet regime, which was initially successful but then collapsed. Assumptions underlying governance by targets are synecdoche (taking a part to stand for a whole) and that problems of measurement and gaming do not matter.[5]

This neo-Soviet character is doubly reinforced when it comes to development aid, where a donor government provides financial aid either bilaterally (to another government) or to multilateral agencies. Typically decisions are made centrally and then programs are delivered on the ground via five-year plans.

The Humanitarian Sphere

In situations of humanitarian disaster, developmental responses are so disrupted by unexpected events (such as natural disasters), that people are suddenly vulnerable to hunger, water shortages, or other emergency challenges. A humanitarian approach then consists of a short-term, rapid response aimed at meeting the immediate needs of shelter, safety, or supply.[6]

Developmental responses, by their close association with governments, are relatively politicized, slow-moving instruments of both domestic and foreign policy. The humanitarian sphere, however, is characterized by underlying principles distinguishing it from other forms of response. In many ways, normal rules are suspended during humanitarian disasters. Foremost are values of neutrality and impartiality. At least in theory, by not taking sides, humanitarian agencies ensure access to war zones and other crisis situations.

Since the 1980s humanitarianism has undergone huge shifts in terms of culture, increasingly being driven by celebrities and global campaigns. In recent years the humanitarian sphere has also come under severe criticism.[7] Formerly apolitical, humanitarian agencies are changing now and "venturing into the formerly taboo area of politics."[8] A challenge comes from the relationship of humanitarian aid and conflict, with accusations being made that in many cases, aid money goes toward supporting conflict.[9] The vast amounts of money at stake in this sphere coupled with its media-saturated culture mean that some critics have christened it "humanitarian business," the harsh point being that this sphere is far from neutral and is actually self-serving.[10]

The Security Sphere

When developmental and humanitarian responses fail, people tend to become desperate, and so a securitized response is called for to contain them. Assuming that developmental and humanitarian responses have failed and that the people suffering act rationally, what will they do in such situations? Faced with imminent risk to their survival, people will respond in one of three ways: (1) fight, (2) leave if possible, or if things get really bad, (3) suffer and potentially lose their lives. This is when securitized responses enter.

In recent years a number of events have changed the nature of security responses: 9-11, the rise of international suicide-martyrdom operations, asymmetrical warfare, and an increase in international protest movements, such as Occupy Wall Street, 15M in Spain, and the Arab Spring. Finally, we are witnessing an exponential rise in international cyber-attacks, which may take the form of criminal activity or even state-versus-state conflict.[11]

When we see riot police or tanks on the streets of a city, we are witnessing a securitized response. According to some scholars, since 9/11 we have seen the rise of "strategic incapacitation" as a security response, focused on the prevention of "crime" through the control of space.[12]

Security is typically containment of grievances. The Troubles in Northern Ireland, the situation of the Palestinians, or the UN presence on the Green Line dividing South and North Cyprus are all examples of long-term securitized responses, where a situation is held in a weird form of attritional stasis for as long as possible. Where this stasis fails, we see battle-space responses, with extreme variability in how successful this strategy is at restoring the peace.

The Battle Sphere

When a security response is deemed insufficient, we are in a situation of war. The last two decades have seen profound changes to the notion of warfare. The so-called Global War on Terror has broken down clear distinctions of who the enemy is, what it means to win a war, and the actual location of the battlefield. Military theorist Emile Simpson comments, "The fact that the military now tends to speak about 'battlespaces' rather than 'battlefields' acknowledges the expansion of the traditional, apolitical, military domain beyond the physical clash of armed forces to include its political, social and economic context even at the local level."[13]

The problems with security and war-as-policy responses are obviously profound. Both are tremendously expensive from every angle. A recent study on the financial legacy of the Iraq and Afghanistan wars show them to be the most expensive wars in US history. Costing between $4 trillion to $6 trillion, "the legacy of decisions taken during the Iraq and Afghanistan wars will dominate future federal budgets for decades to come."[14]

As situations, battle spaces are not amenable to control even as this is the avowed point. They also do little or nothing to address the underlying problems—regime change still leaves a new government with the same challenges on the ground—with the potentially added problem of massive infrastructure loss, internally displaced populations, and the loss of life.

Even as these four spheres retain distinct characteristics, they are blurring. We now see military forces engaged in the humanitarian spheres. We see the distinction between security and battle spaces blurring. In situations such as Afghanistan and Yemen, we see traditional notions of battle making little sense, as there are no set-piece battles.

In some ways, of all four spheres—developmental, humanitarian, security, and battle—it's the battle sphere that is going through the deepest changes. The wars of Iraq and Afghanistan have prompted deep soul-searching in Western militaries. The very notion of strategy in the military sphere is being rethought from the ground up. This is unfortunately not true of other spheres. The historic links of strategy and planning, which are deep, may mean that this re-think has impacts way beyond the military sphere. One of the risks is an increased militarization of other spheres.[15]

THE EXPERT-PLANNING PARADIGM

I was in a nice warm bed. Suddenly I'm part of a plan.
— Woody Allen

BAU responses to complex social challenges start with the formulation of a strategic plan in response to a problem. Different spheres deal with different problems. So, for example, while poverty may play a role in the decision of a young Yemeni picking up a gun, once he does so, he becomes a problem that belongs either to the security or battle sphere. The way the problem's defined or constructed is usually unexamined. It may be inherited from other spheres (e.g., politics or academia) or may simply be a commonly acdepted story.

At the heart of all BAU responses sit experts. They are the muscle behind BAU responses. And what experts do in response to complex social challenges is formulate plans. The formulation of a plan, be it by a development agency or a military commander, leads us to the challenges of implementing the plan. Once a problem domain has clearly been identified (in itself not always obvious) the dominant response is technocratic, a combination of planning and technical problem solving. This is the expert-planning paradigm that drives BAU. It's, unfortunately, profoundly unstrategic in nature and leads to the creation of strategic vacuums coupled with expensive activity around complex social challenges. Vietnam War is a textblook case of this.

According to Henry Mintzberg, a professor who has studied strategic planning extensively, "The act of planning assumes predetermination in the prediction of the environment; the unfolding of the strategy formation process on schedule; and the ability to impose the resulting strategies on an accepting environment." He concludes, "The possibility that formal systems of planning create dynamics which reduce the possibility of truly being strategic or the possibility that planning processes have never really been formal (other than to follow a checklist)."[16]

Mintzberg argues that an expert is "defined as someone who knows enough about a subject to avoid all the many pitfalls on his or her way to the grand fallacy." The grand fallacy is that "no amount of elaboration will ever enable formal procedures to forecast discontinuities, to inform managers who are detached from their operations, to create novel strategies. Ultimately, the term 'strategic planning' has proved to be an oxymoron."[17] In Mintzberg's grand fallacy, the failures of planning are not coincidental but *integral* to the very nature of planning.

In all of this, we have to remember that experts are not politicians; rather they are experts in their particular specialties. This means they make largely rational recommendations, the best of which are characterized by professional integrity.

The trouble is that decisions made by political decision makers are rarely, if ever, made purely on the basis of rationality or common-sense. Rather, they are made on the basis of political expediency, self-interest, and other trade-offs. While rationality is considered in politically loaded decisions, it is not the deciding factor.[18] In other words, if we expect politicians to take the rational recommendations made by well-meaning experts and implement them, then we are living a fantasy.

FLYING AUTOPILOT IN THE PERFECT STORM

One should never bring a knife to a gun fight, nor a cookie cutter to a complex adaptive system.

— Harold Jarche

What I saw at Chatham House was that everyone in the room, every single so-called expert (including me) was playing by the rules and saw little reason to risk breaking them. We were all polite, and few people took a tone that could be called strident or emotional, even though the situation was deeply upsetting.

Part of the reason was, of course, that we believed that no one would listen anyway. And besides, it was unprofessional. At the last meeting I went to, an older Yemeni man, who was in exile, took a somewhat forceful tone arguing passionately against international support for the current regime. While there were murmurs of assent from various people in the room, we swiftly moved on. The Yemeni man settled back into his chair, defeated by a cold politeness. I somehow felt we had all been defeated.

This banishment of messy and potentially embarrassing emotions is one hallmark of the expert-planning paradigm. Mintzberg has summarized these problems as the fallacies of *detachment, predetermination,* and *formalism.*[19] *Detachment* means experts are detached from the situation on the ground and critically have no skin in the game.[20] *Predetermination* means that activities are plotted out in advance, and in the most pernicious instances they do not change, come hell or high water. Finally *formalism* means that if it cannot be measured or somehow expressed on paper, it cannot be taken into consideration.

This results in the creation of vast bureaucratic flatlands—a world of abstract data and reports.[21] Vast representations of reality that are disembodied and exist purely on screens become the place where our decision makers, planners, and donors engage with the reality of their decisions, designs, political power, and resource deployment. These representations costs billions to maintain and constitute a shadow reality that is psychologically, intellectually, technically, and physically much easier to deal with than reality itself. The disembodiment of reality is buried within cold, emotionless, antiseptic language, and technical processes, in "mathematical condensations of wounded images of a life worth living." Consider the saying often attributed to Stalin that one death is a tragedy, but a million deaths is statistics.[22]

Ultimately, taking a planning-based approach in situations of complexity is akin to flying a plane on autopilot in a raging storm. Autopilot is an elegant technology that allows for long-distance flight. Flying on autopilot means that the plane keeps flying as long as the hardware and software of the autopilot are functioning within the limits for which they were designed. In other words, autopilots are not designed to fly in all weather conditions. When a storm surrounds a plane or when some other unforeseen event arises, human beings have to step in to make decisions, or inevitably the plane crashes.

A LACK OF GENUINE STRATEGIC INTENT

> In the beginner's mind there are many possibilities, but in the expert's there are few.
> — Shunryu Suzuki

What is it that causes us to approach challenges on autopilot? The French sociologist Pierre Bourdieu offers us an explanation through his idea of *habitus*.[23] This idea provides us with an understanding of BAU and why we "keep doing what we've always done." For Bourdieu, habitus is much more than habit; it is "long-lasting dispositions of the mind and body," that he sees as "a product of history." It's the way we think, talk, dress, work, and live our everyday lives in repeating patterns.

Habitus is like muscle memory. If we perform the same task over and over again, like riding a bicycle, then our muscles remember the actions without our conscious mind being a part of the act. In military training, repetition is used to train soldiers in tasks such as disassembling a weapon, so that when they are under pressure, their muscles can automatically perform the task without the mind having to think about it. Habitus is used to overcome the natural fight-or-flight response that arises in moments of extreme crisis. The systems built around training soldiers, in particular, illustrate habitus.

In other words, there are whole systems designed to reinforce particular behaviors through rewarding repetition. Such systems over time would produce habitus and would not require coercion, rules, or laws; it would just be that way. This ensures the "active presence of past experiences," which "tend to guarantee the 'correctness' of practices and their constancy over time, more reliably than all formal rules and explicit norms."[24]

BAU strategies are unsuited to complex social challenges because they are not the product of what Bourdieu calls "genuine strategic intention," oriented toward current realities and the emerging future. Rather, BAU stems from habitus that is "the source of these strings of 'moves,' which are objectively organized as strategies without being the product of genuine strategic intention—which would presuppose at least that they be apprehended as one among other possible strategies."

A particular strategy originating from habitus can give the impression of being strategic, that is, formulated in response to a challenge. Instead, what we have are strategies that are created in advance of the objective conditions they purport to be responding to. In other words, they are pseudo-strategies.

I recall an example of this at one meeting where I was introduced to an expert with the comment that he might have useful ideas for our work in Yemen. I explained what we were doing and looked at him expectantly. He told me, "You need to think about these things . . ." and proceeded to explain various commodity supply chains to me. When he finished, I asked him, "So, can I see the data that your analysis is based on?" He looked at me, surprised, and said, "Oh no, this is just standard political economy stuff." The actual situation in Yemen and its trajectory didn't factor into his advice.

At worst, an expert-planning response involves a menu of pre-configured answers, as opposed to a completely new strategy that a completely new situation might demand. At best, an expert is a good guide to a narrow domain of historical practice. This service is valuable—experts have been thinking longer and harder than other people about their domains. However, the expert strategic response based on habitus is based on the past of what was acceptable practice.

Our reliance on the expert-planning paradigm is an example of Bourdieu's observation, "Practice has a logic which is not that of the logician."[25] This means that when faced with a real need to adapt our behaviors to a new reality, we as a society are unable to do so. Decision-making power and the control of resources rests with a narrow class of technocrats occupying BAU spaces, characterized by habitus. In the face of increasingly complex social challenges, this results in a troubling strategic vacuum masked by frantic technocratic activity.

3

The Sustainable Food Lab: From Farm to Fork

How and what we eat determines to a great extent the use we make of this world—and what is to become of it.

— Michael Pollen, *The Omnivore's Dilemma: A Natural History of Four Meals*

One sign of *genuine strategic intent* is doing things because we personally think it's a good idea, as opposed to doing something because we are told to. At Generon I found genuine strategic intent in abundance. Behind a relatively conservative front, I found myself part of a tiny group that had taken upon itself a mission to address "ten global problems in ten years." No one had asked us to undertake this mission and we had no authority from anyone to take it on.[1]

The means of undertaking this mission was called the *change lab*. Change labs are first-generation social labs. They're prototypes because they draw on a relatively narrow base of approaches, whereas next-generation social labs draw on a much wider range. During the life of Generon, several change labs were attempted.

The core idea of the change lab came from *Leadership in the Dig-*

ital Economy, coauthored by Joseph Jaworksi and Otto Scharmer.[2] They argued that "doing well in the new economy requires the enhancement of a particular capacity: the ability to sense and actualize emerging realities." The lab from its very first conception was concerned less with planning and more with emergence.

In a change lab, a group of stakeholders work to surface their own ideas for what will effectively shift a system from its current unacceptable state to a desired future state. The change lab starts by bringing participants together around a broadly defined area, usually represented by a question. We call this activity *convening*. The question has to be sufficiently broad to appeal to a wide group of stakeholders and sufficiently open as to allow people to pursue multiple directions in addressing the challenge they are concerned with.

Over the course of a change lab, this diverse group goes through a common journey, which in broad strokes consists of seeing the system with their own eyes, connecting to their own personal commitments, and quickly prototyping seed initiatives on the ground. These phases of activity—called Sensing, Presencing, and Realizing—are drawn directly from the U Process,[3] an innovation process that informs the underlying architecture of first-generation social labs.[4]

During my time at Generon I was principally involved in three change labs: the Sustainable Food Lab, the Bhavishya Lab, and one focused on aboriginal issues in Canada, which was prompted by a series of teenage suicides in a community off Vancouver Island. Although we worked with the First Nations and other stakeholders on this issue for many years, this effort was unsuccessful. One of the issues was the definition of the problem we inherited—that aboriginal communities were the problem that needed to be fixed.

The habitus at the heart of this challenge was many centuries old: most responses to the challenges faced by aboriginal communities were built on reconstituting the status quo. Almost every attempt we made to evolve away from the status quo was blocked. I still struggle with this failure, thinking often about the communities we worked with and pondering our role and what we might have done differently.

THE RACE TO THE BOTTOM

The story of the modern global food system is the story of unintended consequences. It's the story of a causal logic run amok. It's the familiar story of how we're all intimately connected without quite grasping just how intimately. It's the deeply disturbing story of a system characterized by historic injustice that continues to produce injustice today. It's a story that goes to the throbbing, bleeding heart of sustainability. It can, without being hyperbolic, be called the mother of all systemic problems.

Food is perhaps the first complex challenge humanity has faced. From our time as hunter-gatherers through the era of modern mega-farms, we have struggled to figure out how to feed ourselves. The modern food system somewhat magically supports a world population that our ancestors would have found unimaginable. Agriculture is the largest industry on the planet, employing an estimated 1.3 billion people.[5] And prophecies of its collapse are as old as writing. Famine is a specter that has haunted humanity for ten thousand years, as far back as the invention of agriculture.

The world's population is projected to grow from its current 6.5 billion to 9.2 billion by 2050.[6] World food production probably needs to double in the coming decades.[7] This has enormous implications. The expansion of agricultural activity as currently practiced would severely impact already-stressed natural resources. Agriculture and livestock production use about half of the habitable land on Earth, which doesn't even include vast quantities of water and fossil fuels.

If world food production does not grow fast enough—given that one billion people on the planet go hungry today (despite there being technically enough food in the world to feed them)— what will it mean to add three billion more? The question isn't simply how to feed the world population; the question is how to feed all of us in such a way that we don't simply degrade our ecosystems to the point where they collapse under us.

Food is necessary for life. This means that market-oriented approaches to supplying food are problematic. From a pure market-oriented point of view, high demand for scarce resources is a recipe for high prices and high profit margins. This formula for profit is fine when we're dealing with a non-subsistence commodity, such as an iPad—no one will die if its demand far exceeds supply and its price goes through the roof. But when food is treated as a commodity, all sorts of issues arise.

One key problem in a market-oriented food system is the issue of factoring in what economists have come to call *externalities*, that is, the environmental costs associated with producing food. An often-cited example of this involves factoring in all the environmental costs (the cost of water being a big part) of a Big Mac from McDonald's. Instead of costing a few dollars, it would cost a few hundred dollars.[8] The fact that the consumer is not paying for these externalities raises the question: who *will* pay for them? Typically such resources are extracted from the commons, hence the expression "tragedy of the commons."

Due to changing lifestyle choices (more people want to eat meat) and increases in population, the demand for food is growing, which creates a race to the bottom where meeting demand through strictly market mechanisms will lead to the eventual collapse of our ecosystems.

The goal then is to figure out what *sustainable food* actually looks like, that is, food that's sustainable from multiple angles—from environmental to financial. How is it possible to meet the world's food needs while maintaining a healthy planet? This is the question at the heart of the Sustainable Food Lab.

THE MULTIPLE AND CONFLICTING LOGICS OF FOOD

What is sustainable is most intriguing for me. Sustainable agriculture for a rural population of two billion is one thing, for six billion evenly divided [between rural and urban] is another and for nine billion, which is mostly urban, is an entirely different thing. You don't solve that—no matter how big you are—alone.

— Food Lab Champion[9]

Through a grindingly painful process I realized that there actually isn't a single overriding logic guiding the global food system. Rather, there are multiple, conflicting, and sometimes faulty theories, profoundly disconnected from each other, that contribute to its incredible complexity. Where these theories *do* meet, more often than not, the engagement is violent, with supporters of different beliefs seeking to exploit, delegitimize, or even destroy the other.

The Food Lab grew out of a breakfast conversation in 2002. That breakfast, in some ways, was decades in the making. It brought together four people who represented different approaches in handling complex social problems that had been maturing for many years.

The first was Hal Hamilton, a farmer and a long-time food

activist. He had decades of experience, relationships, and focus on the sustainability of the food system. Don Seville, who worked with Hal, and Peter Senge represented systems thinking, a school of thought associated with Donella Meadows, one of the authors of *Limits to Growth*. Meadows first articulated the idea that the planet had a limited "carrying capacity" in terms of how many people it could support.[10]

Finally, there was my colleague Adam Kahane from Generon. Adam, for all intents and purposes, represented the change lab, an approach that was new to the scene and potentially offered an alternate path to the well-understood problem of sustaining global food systems.

The breakfast conversation "started exploring the possibility that the polarized debates over agricultural sustainability might benefit from the application of the 'U' method, which offers a process to foster breakthrough thinking and action on complex, cross-sector problems. The conversation later expanded to include Andre van Heemstra, Jan Kees Vis, and Jeroen Bordewijk of Unilever and Oran Hesterman of the Kellogg Foundation."[11]

The Food Lab launched in 2004 in the Netherlands, after almost two years of work by the original breakfast group and others. It started as a two-year process, with some thirty-odd participants (called lab team members). Funding came mainly from the Kellogg Foundation with smaller amounts contributed from a number of other donors.

When I started working with Generon, the Food Lab was on the verge of launching. Even so, the exact constitution of the participants had not been finalized. In particular, the focus was on bringing in the corporate sector and ensuring adequate representation from a group that clearly formed a major part of the global food system. Without corporate sector participation, the

Food Lab was arguably dead in the water because of the key role it played in the global food system.

Unilever was a major supporter of the Food Lab. Antony Burgmans, the Chairman of Unilever at the time, was what we called a *champion*. Jan Kees Vis, then a Sustainable Agriculture Manager for Unilever, participated as a lab team member and, in subsequent years, became a key champion of the lab. He also emerged as a driving force in Unilever's ambitious attempts to source all its supplies from sustainable providers.

Before the lab launched, frantic negotiations and calls were being made to increase corporate participation. This effort by and large succeeded. The interesting thing I observed about corporate sector participation was how fragile it seemed and how much fear there was around the corporations walking out.

At the launch meeting of the Food Lab I was cautioned against recommending any reading to the participants—anything that might jeopardize their participation, especially literature critical of the global food system. (Interestingly, the readings listed in official lab documentation were mostly written by climate-change skeptics and defenders of industrial agriculture, with no references to the vast literature critiquing industrial agriculture.) This attitude within the support team, called the lab secretariat, was offset by the noncorporate sector participants, who initially included a broad spectrum of people critical of the growing corporatization of the food sector.

Everything about the Food Lab was carefully constructed. It consisted of a series of physical gatherings and workshops, which brought lab team members together to go through a shared innovation process, built on the U Process.

The venue for launching the Lab and its first workshop was the Blooming Hotel in Bergen, situated on the Dutch coast, off the North Sea. The hotel had been a folk school, a key education movement in the Netherlands and Scandinavian countries that provided a practical education for the children of farmers.

The focus of the change lab was "on practical initiatives, beginning with new or improved food supply chains, developed as a central focus of the Food Lab from the determination expressed by many [lab members] to make change 'on the ground' through practical action, pilot projects and viable full-scale food system interventions."[12] The hotel's history echoed and mirrored the practical aspirations of the Food Lab.

WHAT IS SUSTAINABLE?

Eugenio Peixoto, Secretary of Agrarian Reform from Brazil, at the opening session of the lab, spoke powerfully about the issue of food equity. He spoke about "food apartheid" where consumers in the Global South were forced to eat genetically modified, processed, unhealthy food because it was all they could afford, while in the Global North consumers were able to eat organic, wholesome food at reasonable prices. These voices were critical to the lab. They provided the space allowing for more honest and deeper conversations.

Three characteristics about the lab struck me as novel and were likely unfamiliar to the participants. The first was the constitution of the lab team, that is, the core participants. This was a very diverse multi-stakeholder peer group. While groups can always be more diverse, the initial constitution of the lab brought together a wide range of organizational representation, political positions, and geographies, coupled with a relatively good gender balance. The rule of thumb behind the constitution of the lab team was "diverse and influential." This idea came straight from

Adam's work with scenario planning and, in particular, the success of convening diverse participants for the Mont Fleur process in South Africa.[13]

The second novel aspect of the lab was the lack of a predetermined set of outcomes. The strategic goals of the lab were stated in various ways, but they were largely fuzzy. These included statements of purpose, such as "The purpose of the Sustainable Food Lab is to accelerate the movement of sustainably produced food from niche to mainstream" and "By 2018, the majority of the food bought and sold around the world is in a sustainability program in which such improvement is planned and measured." This fuzziness served to bring a diverse group together because participants could interpret the strategic goals in their own way. A more formalized and quantitatively precise set of goals would interest a narrower set of stakeholders, thus reducing diversity.

The core process that the lab was built on, the U Process, largely eschews predetermined and planned outcomes in favor of *emergent* outcomes. Part of our challenge as a secretariat was to convince participants that there was a genuine openness to outcomes, that the process had not been gamed in any way, with the conveners and the secretariat pushing some secret agenda.

This was another reason for caution in disseminating any material that would betray the biases of the secretariat. The emergent nature of the process was very different from a purely planned approach, where sets of outcomes are exhaustively defined, usually by a single problem owner, and then the task becomes execution. This approach would not work with a diverse group for a number of reasons. If a single problem owner were to define the goals and strategy, then, by definition, this ownership would not be shared, and the probability of alignment with diverse stakeholders goes down. So from a very pragmatic point of view, both the fuzziness of the goals and the emergent nature of the process allowed for the convening of a diverse group. This did not mean that everyone was comfortable with that openness.

Indeed, on the very first day of the lab there was an outcry over the lack of formal definitions. Participants demanded that the secretariat define the term *sustainable*. Since this was the Sustainable Food Lab, what was the definition of the word? Members of the secretariat, by luck, insight, and belief, held up their hands, telling the participants that it was up to them to define the word, and reminding them that this was day one of a two-year process. We thus avoided a common trap in diverse gatherings, of getting bogged down in futile debates about language. In time, participants gained an understanding that multiple definitions of the word *sustainable* were prevalent across the system and, of course, within the lab itself.

The most interesting part of the first day for me was the exercise in which we asked people to bring two objects, one more sustainable and one less. That exercise brought out all the group's diversity in startling color. One corporate participant had some Kraft and RJ Reynolds Lunchable pizzas as his unsustainable product. He called it a "product abomination" because it was marketed to kids and their parents as a healthy product, and, in fact, it was the exact opposite.

One of the French participants had cheese from eastern France, produced by farmers in little cooperatives, as his more sustainable product. To my surprise, he had picked a box of raw cane sugar from Brazil as his less-sustainable product. He explained that it was unsustainable because 800,000 Brazilians labored to produce it under really terrible conditions and to import such a product was a joke. I noticed Eugenio keeping a poker face and one of the other Brazilians sort of going red in the face—but neither said anything.

Afterward we were standing at the tables looking at the products, and Antony Burgmans from Unilever was looking through the less sustainable ones. He innocently picked up the cane sugar and asked why it was less sustainable. The red-faced Brazilian from earlier was standing next to him, and he started snarling about it. I mentioned the 800,000 workers as Burgmans beat a hasty retreat. The Brazilian mumbled something about "fucking Frenchman" and said, "Zaid, come to Brazil and I'll take you and show you the cane plantations and we'll see what's what." And he did.

This leads us to another novel aspect of the lab. The first part of the Change Lab, drawing on the U Process, involved participants suspending their pet strategies and focusing their energies on understanding the current reality of the global food system. In other words, for this part of the process at least, what the participants believed or wanted mattered less than understanding what already was. While the participants might want a single definition of the word *sustainable,* the reality, whether they liked it or not, was that the word had multiple definitions and there were in fact *multiple realities.*

These definitions could be observed. When we took participants on a learning journey to visit an organic coffee processor in the Netherlands, they understood *sustainable* to mean environmental sustainability. When we visited a multimillion-dollar sugar cane grower and manufacturer in Minas Gerais, Brazil, they understood it to mean *financial* sustainability rather than environmental or cultural.

These skills of suspending had to be learned, and they proved to be initially challenging for a number of participants. One senior EU policy advisor, on being told that she had to "suspend judgment," asked in disbelief, "For thirty years, I've been paid to exercise my judgment, and you want me to stop?" Another participant told us that he was not some yogi and that it was an impossible request. The learning journeys we ran in order to understand the global food system in time became one of the most enduring parts of the Food Lab.

The lab in practice was a negotiated space where strategy was concerned. While the process was fixed, in some ways rigidly so, the strategies that the lab team could execute were entirely open. Part of my challenge was therefore to grasp what it is that the lab team members were negotiating over.

SYSTEMIC SPREAD BETTING

> Innovation is always a numbers game: the more of it you do, the better your chances of reaping a fat payoff.
>
> — Gary Hamel, *The Future of Management*

What turned out to be perhaps the most critical workshop of the lab took place in the unlikely surroundings of the Schloss Leopoldskron. The Schloss is a palace in Salzburg, Austria, built in 1736, with a dramatic history. Framed by a little lake and the snow-capped northern edge of the Alps, it's also the building where *The Sound of Music* was filmed.

In these grandiose surroundings, the lab team members firmed up the pilot projects that they were to undertake over the coming year. They devised six initiatives, which included sustainable fisheries, smallholder farms in Latin America, responsible commodities, and a business coalition for sustainability.

The initiatives had been decided at the previous workshop, so we entered the Schloss with ideas for what each of them would look like. The task now was to flesh them out and start prototyping them as quickly as possible.

The workshop was fraught with tension, partly because we had decided to open up membership of the lab. Almost thirty new people joined the lab at this point. This had a major impact on the quality of trust and shared understanding in the room. We struggled mightily to hold the integrity of the lab together to avoid having to start again.

In working on these issues and reflecting on the nature of the challenge that the lab was confronting, I came to some realizations about the nature of the work. The first is that social labs are not projects. A project has a beginning and an end. Project-like thinking has been the dominant approach to addressing societal challenges. Doug Reeler, from the South African organization Community Development Resource Association (CDRA), remarks on the trend toward "projectization" in development:

> The relationship between Governments, donors, NGOs, CBOs, growing legions of freelance international development consultants, private companies and even some social movements is increasingly being shaped by this trend of putting Projects to tender, paying people as service providers to achieve centrally determined outcomes. . . . Development funding is fast becoming a marketplace governed by tender processes and business-talk.[14]

Reeler observes one of the deeper consequences of this: "Short-term Projects are effectively replacing established organizations as implementing vehicles."

While a lab is sometimes referred to as a "platform for innovation," it is perhaps easiest to think of the Food Lab as a new type of organization, a multi-stakeholder institution. It is a platform for innovation, but it aspires to be a stable platform—not one that will go away after a few years. Projects therefore, emerge from the platform. Some of them are successful and some of them are not. The work of the institution is to generate a constant stream of innovations.

These innovations can be understood as a form of *systemic spread betting*. Since we don't know in advance what will work to change or shift a system, we spread our bets, much in the same way a venture capitalist will spread risk by betting on a range of start-ups in the hope that at least a few will succeed. In fact, it's fairly well understood by VCs that most of their investments will fail.

The lab process generated an initial portfolio of initiatives. Some of these initiatives started and ended, some of them succeeded and continued, while some of them failed. The point is that the Sustainable Food Lab acted like an engine for generating new innovations. That doesn't mean, of course, all the innovations coming from the Food Lab will succeed. As any Silicon Valley insider, venture capitalist, or innovator will tell you, innovation arises from a community of people focused on trying out lots of things and learning their way to successful innovations.

The nature of complex social challenges means that perhaps, more than anything, what is required is a stable platform, an institution that can bring together diverse capital, talent, and strategic direction to build collaborative responses. It also means that the challenge is highly unlikely to simply go away. Humankind has suffered hunger, poverty, and injustice for its entire history. It would be, at the very least, hubristic to think that we are about to completely eradicate these challenges from the human condition.

How is it possible to meet the world's food needs while maintaining a healthy planet? When first confronted with this question at the heart of the Food Lab, I didn't appreciate the absurdity or difficulty of the challenge. The more I learned about food systems, the more the question felt to me like a koan.

In Zen practice, a koan is a particular type of question that, on the face of it, seems not to make any sense. It's used with students to provoke great doubt and gauge their progress in Zen.

For example, "Two hands clap and there is a sound. What is the sound of one hand?" The more I pondered the question at the heart of the lab, the more paradoxical and problematic it seemed. From a pragmatic point of view, however, the value of a koan is not in answering the question, for there is no answer. It's that the Zen student, in struggling with the question, arrives at a new way of being, valuing, if you like, the very nature of the struggle. The struggle generates value, producing new insights and change. Treating a koan like a project is a recipe for failure.

Hal and Don continue to lead both old and new lab team members in a productive struggle to come to grips with the koan at the heart of the lab. Almost ten years since the first workshop in Bergen, the Food Lab is going strong.

4

The Bhavishya Lab:
The Silent Emergency

The Indian experiment is still in its early stages, and its outcome may well turn out to be the most significant of them all, partly because of its sheer human scale, and partly because of its location, a substantial bridgehead of effervescent liberty on the Asian continent.

— Sunil Khilani

The Indian experiment in democracy is the largest in the world. A billion people and counting means that Indian challenges are staggering in sheer human scale. It is hard to get beyond the numbers. Forty-seven percent of India's 414 million children under the age of six have some form of malnutrition.

My participation in the Food Lab led me to the next lab we undertook, the Bhavishya Alliance, focused on child malnutrition in India. We described the challenge as follows:

Malnutrition is a complex issue to tackle because it's a multi-factoral phenomenon. Because there is no one single cause, the factors that effect the situation are diverse and difficult to tackle in parallel. . . . The situation is seemingly intractable, partly due to the increase in the absolute number of children being born, partly due to the complex nature of the change required at multiple levels (from the mother through to governmental institutions) and finally as a consequence of the size and diversity of India's population and geography.

Part of me was obviously excited about the work and wanted to plunge in. Another part of me saw this as an intervention very different from the Sustainable Food Lab and wanted to have nothing to do with it. The scope of the Food Lab was global, and there were no beneficiaries being directly targeted. *Bhavishya*, meaning *future* in Sanskrit, was a stark contrast. It ended up, after much debate, being focused on one state in India, Maharashtra, with a population of 80 million, and its key beneficiaries were to be children under the age of six suffering from malnutrition.

These strategic decisions of scope and focus put Bhavishya squarely in the space of international development. With my background, having partly grown up in India and all four of my grandparents being originally Indian, I had a strange insider-outsider understanding of the context. Unlike the Food Lab, where I had entered with little understanding of the nature of the challenges, I had a much deeper understanding of the waters we were about to enter into. I knew they were deep enough to drown in.

A significant part of my discomfort was that the whole initiative originated outside India. The key funder and driver behind Bhavishya was Unilever, and in particular, Tex Gunning, who was Dutch. Tex and Joseph Jaworski (one of the other founders of Generon Consulting) had together dreamed up a major intervention in the area of child malnutrition.[1]

The very idea of an initiative cooked up at a conference in Finland by a Dutch man (Tex) and Texan (Joseph), involving no Indians, funded by one of the largest multinational corporations in the world, was problematic from multiple angles. And it was giving me sleepless nights.

A few weeks after arriving in India, I passed through Surat, in Gujarat. Even at midnight, the brightly lit central train station was a crazed, frantic mass of people: food vendors, passengers sleeping on the floor of the station, and dogs trotting around merrily scavenging. Outside, multiple lanes of nonstop traffic whooshed around, honking, braking hard, and in perpetual motion. It felt like being on the edge of a tidal wave of people, cars, and blinding lights.

As I walked into the station, I heard a shout and turned to see a grown man with red eyes lunge at a young boy, aged maybe nine or ten, dressed in shorts and a dirty T-shirt. The boy, clearly startled, lurched backward but not fast enough to avoid a hard, booming punch to the chest. His eyes opened wide in shock and surprise, as he clutched his chest and stumbled back, trying to stay on his feet. He turned and ran as the man lumbered half-heartedly after him, swearing that he would kill him. The man stopped after a few steps and caught me staring at him, my mouth open. He looked down sullenly and shuffled off.

Over coffee, I recounted to my Indian colleague what I had seen. She shrugged and told me to get over it, that it wasn't possible to intervene in every little act of violence I witnessed. For me, the experience gave rise to a multitude of questions. At first, I found myself wondering why I hadn't intervened, why I hadn't said something. Then I wondered at the violence that I kept witnessing in Indian society. Did the little boy run off and find a still littler boy to take it out on? Was there really wisdom to "getting used to it"? I remembered a line I had read somewhere: "We have been defeated twice. We no longer protest, not even inwardly."

My ambivalence toward the effort plagued me. My reluctance

stemmed from my complicated relationship with India, which I could not reconcile. On the one hand, I loved it—its people, its food, and its vastness. On the other hand, I struggled mightily against manifestations of India that just seemed unbelievably cruel and how bystanders just shrugged. I often felt I was fighting the tide in India.

THE BHAVISHYA ALLIANCE

From the initial conception in early 2003 to the launch of the lab in 2006 was three years of hard work. During this time a vast array of strategic options were explored: where exactly the lab would take place and how long it would run for. In-depth research on child malnutrition was conducted.

In the year before the lab, we began working with a partner organization, the Synergos Institute, and put our collective shoulders to the wheel in order to prepare. The work ranged from high-level negotiations with the government and key champions to designing a new workshop space from scratch that would fit one hundred people. We interviewed potential staff members, contracted delivery partners, and set up the necessary legal structures.

Almost one hundred painstaking in-person interviews were conducted in India, with stakeholders across the board, in a number of different states. These interviews allowed us to get a very broad understanding of what was happening and, most critically, who was up for doing what. All major decisions were informed by the interviews, including the decision of which state the lab would focus on and which organizations and individuals were invited to participate. The most time-consuming parts were mapping out the field of stakeholders and then negotiating participation with over fifty organizations—some of which joined the lab, but some did not.

The strategic response marshaled against the challenge of child malnutrition in India eventually brought together almost thirty organizations as part of the lab team and another thirty-odd organizations as champions and supporters. Whereas with the Food Lab, we had run a somewhat leisurely process over two years, the feedback had been that this was too long. This time we were looking at a six-month process, which was later shortened to an intense three-month process.

Participants were seconded to the lab, with three weeks on and one week off for three months. We designed the lab in ten modules of a week each. These modules included a launch week; community learning journeys, in which the lab team traveled in six sub-teams to the five target districts, where they undertook disciplined observation of the system from the perspectives of frontline actors and of communities, parents, and children; a nature retreat in a remote wilderness location in Uttaranchal, in order to reflect individually and collectively on what they were being called to do and where they were to focus their energies; and then three weeks of prototyping initiatives.

For a long time, figuring out how to involve the government of India was a puzzle. Then we met V. Ramani, the director general of the Rajmata Jijau Mother-Child Health and Nutrition Mission, the state-level apparatus responsible for the issue of child malnutrition in Maharashtra. Ramani was a senior Indian civil servant who reported to the Minister for Women and Child Development. The goals of the lab and the mission aligned almost perfectly. Ramani immediately understood the lab's potential and arranged for a number of participants from a diverse range of government organizations to participate.

There were key differences between participants in the Food Lab and Bhavishya. Whereas the Food Lab team was composed of peers, there was vast diversity among the Bhavishya participants. They ranged from someone recently granted a PhD in nutrition to a senior government grandee on the verge of retirement.

MK Sharmer, one of the champions of the lab from Hindustan Lever, explained to us what the lab means for India: "We are engaged in a truly historic endeavour within the Indian context." Sharmer stated that in sixty years, "India has never attempted to address a social challenge of this magnitude utilizing a tri-sector partnership as a primary problem-solving methodology."[2]

We hired a number of Indian facilitators to join the core team a few weeks before the lab started. The secretariat was almost half the size of the core lab team, so when the full contingent of champions was there, we sometimes had over one hundred people in the room.

THE MOON SHOT

By the time Bhavishya launched on April 10, 2006, in Aurangabad, I had undergone a two-year crash course in the complexity of the global food system through my involvement in the Food Lab. I arrived brimming with anxiety. While many of its parameters had been fixed before I joined the team, there were still many decisions to be made. Although the Generon team had all kinds of experience, I was the only person on the team with any experience in grassroots development. I was also the only one on the international team who knew India (as much as India can be known) and who could speak one of its major languages. Yet I was still the most junior member of the team in a system that was quite hierarchical.

As we formally opened the proceedings, one of the conversations I had with my colleagues was about how much of a honeymoon phase we would have with the participants before they felt comfortable enough to challenge the process. We thought maybe we'd get a week. As it turned out, challenges started surfacing within twenty-four hours. They were to continue over the next three months, growing in frequency and ferocity as time passed.

We decided to build a group yoga exercise into our day. We dutifully checked, and one of our Indian facilitators assured us that it was completely fine. What could be more Indian than yoga?

On the second day, one of the participants asked to speak to me. We found a quiet corner. He explained to me that he was Christian and felt extremely uncomfortable practicing yoga with the whole group. So I asked the participant what his concerns were.

The participant explained that one of the facilitators, the same one who had assured us it was fine, had prior to the exercise sung a *bhajan*, which is a Hindu religious song. He was concerned that he was taking part in a Hindu religious exercise, and that made him feel uncomfortable. I was somewhat dumbfounded but could see his point. I assured him that we were not asking him to participate in a religious ceremony and that many people all over the world do yoga that are not Hindu. I said I'd raise it with the team and get back to him. When I did, the Indians, all of whom were Hindu, basically told me to tell him to get over it.

I scratched my head over this little problem. While it was hardly serious, the whole point of the energy practice was to help align the Lab Team as a whole. If one person sat out on day two, how many more would object and demand to sit out? Being religious, I could sympathize and couldn't see myself telling him to get over it.

Despite finding a copy of *Yoga for Christians* online, we couldn't convince the team member to participate, so we dropped the yoga.

Instead, team members decided that they would start each day by singing, in true Indian fashion with huge feeling, a popular national rendition of "We Shall Overcome."

For the second week, we split the group into six sub-teams and took them to live in communities that were suffering from malnutrition. I took one group to a small village called Narmada Nagar, which I had visited previously as part of the pre-launch prep. The village was relatively new and housed refugees from areas flooded by the controversial Narmada Dam. Despite huge grassroots support, the fight against the big dam was lost. These people, with their malnourished children, were just one effect of that.

Initially, a number of the participants complained about having to sleep in a village. Some of the government participants said that they had been to thousands of villages. Some of them were concerned about having to sleep outside. One of them had a little temper tantrum when he discovered we would be eating the same way the villagers ate. They had one meal a day. He tried to convince me to drive the jeep four hours to the nearest town so that he could get breakfast.

Eventually though, everyone settled down. People were sleeping better than they had in a long time, as the night air was cool and fresh. The villagers were very hospitable and friendly. It was hard not to relax and discuss what we were trying to do in such surroundings.

We quickly discovered the real nature of the challenge. The night before we arrived, a child had died from a snakebite. He had gone out with his father to irrigate the crops in the middle of the night. In the dark he got bitten and died. We wondered why they were irrigating the fields at night. It turned out they got only a few hours of electricity every twenty-four hours, and it was in the middle of the night, so that is when they had to pump water into the fields.

The next day we were also shown a modern clinic in the village. Someone asked what was in the white cupboard. "Ah, that cupboard holds antidotes to snake bite venom" was the response. We couldn't understand why a child had died when snakebite kits were less than a hundred meters from his house. Apparently the doctor had left, locking up the place, and no one knew where he was. As we walked out of the clinic, we noticed that all the outside lights were broken, and shards of glass lay on the dust around the clinic. We found out that people had been stoning the clinic and smashing all the lights whenever new ones were put in. These were some of the paradoxes we confronted from our first-person experience with the system.

Then one night before bed, one of the participants who worked for a bank told me the story of how she was recruited to the lab. Her boss had called her to tell her about this opportunity and asked if she was interested. She said no, but her boss told her to think about it. She did. When her boss called again, she reaffirmed the no, saying she was much too busy to take three months out and she felt it would harm her career. Her boss went silent for a minute and then told her if she wanted to keep her job, she had to sign up. So she signed up.

I nearly fell off my string-bed. Part of me couldn't believe my ears. Another part of me was unsurprised. In my experience, Indian organizations were run on rigid hierarchical lines. Our process required people to be self-selected and willingly undertake the process. Later on, I learned that all of our government participants had simply been given marching orders to turn up to the lab via a diktat from above. Some were not even told how long they would be gone for.

The dynamics within the lab were challenging. It was very difficult to discern where people were coming from. The lab team, in many ways, was stuck between the secretariat—who was running the process—and the champions. In the Food Lab, the participants had all been senior figures in their own organizations and outnumbered the champions; in Bhavishya, the situation was dramatically different. There were more champions than participants, and a number of people who turned up to champion meetings had no representation in the lab team.

In the third week of the lab, participants presented early ideas for initiatives to a large and somewhat rowdy group of champions, who followed up with negative reactions, critiques, and a lack of inquiry. To be fair to them, there was a conversation that needed to happen that did not—a conversation about what the champions thought of the lab itself. Instead, they were invited to comment on ideas that the participants came up with. This meant that their overall reactions to the lab so far were channeled through comments made about what the participants were doing. In other words, far from being the supportive *champions* who were helpful to the lab team, they were critics, playing an attacking role. The lab team was extremely upset with the champions, with us, and with themselves. This dynamic was to continue unabated throughout the life of the lab.

Another reason for this dynamic was that many lab team members were hierarchically junior and working not in management or strategic roles but in frontline roles. As far as innovation was concerned, this was great, as they brought in a practical understanding of the challenges on the ground. However, in a society where organizational culture is deeply hierarchical, this was problematic. The innovation process, in other words, was profoundly and deeply distorted by opaque political processes. In the official learning history for the lab, we analyzed this dynamic by looking at *hidden transcripts*, or essential conversations that people deemed too risky to have in public.[3] The power dynamics within the lab swung wildly. It is hard to appreciate how debilitating this was until one experienced it personally.

MOVEMENT REQUIRES FRICTION

A wheel turns because of its encounter with the surface of a road; spinning in the air it goes no where. Rubbing two sticks together produces heat and light; one stick alone is just a stick. As a metaphorical image, friction reminds us that heterogeneous and unequal encounters can lead to new arrangements of culture and power.

— Anna Lowenhaupt Tsing, *Friction: An Ethnography of Global Connection*

As part of my secretariat duties, I produced a report on our visit to Narmada Nager. In it was buried a comment that was interpreted as accusing the government participants of sleeping on the job. The report was an amalgamation of several sets of notes, and for a while, I didn't know who had written the comment. Between the time that report was circulated and I got the original notes back, the lab team had become a bit of a lynch mob.

The lab team demanded that we "hand over" the author of the offending comment so that he or she could be "dealt with." When we discussed the issue, all the participants from the government sat together in a block facing the rest of the group. At their head was the most senior government figure. He called upon people in his group to speak and shushed them when he thought they had said enough. It felt like a court.

With the discovery a few weeks later that I was the author of the offending comment, a half-hearted effort was made to punish me. I was *persona non grata* for a week, to the point where my ability to perform my role was being compromised. In response, my colleagues, Adam and Joe, stepped in and flatly declared their support for me. After some feedback and complaining, I was "rehabilitated."

Gomathy, our learning historian, remarked in a team debrief on how Adam and Joe had stepped up for me. Then she pointed out the same thing had happened to her, but none of us had stepped up for her. She had effectively been ignored by much of the lab team for weeks because of a comment she made about gender. It was a deeply sobering moment—one of many home truths.

At this point we had returned from a weeklong nature retreat in the Himalayas where participants had clarified their commitments and also come up with the initiatives they wanted to pilot. A number of sub-teams were formed. We began the process of testing and prototyping their ideas.

The nature of the prototyping process, when done well, makes it a very different approach from a planning process, one that causes real cognitive dissonance in planning-oriented cultures. As we headed into the final crunch point of the lab—the final presentations to a sub-set of champions called a *venture committee*—prototyping devolved into classic planning.

Due to a lack of clarity about roles and power dynamics, we did not stop to agree on the prototypes with the ultimate clients—the champions. We made several attempts to get buy-in from champions, but in our rush, we did not craft a tightly contracted agreement, which made our attempts seem more like consultation. In other words, champions were happy to verbally give input, but that didn't mean they agreed. And it certainly did not mean they had devolved authority. We inadvertently slid into a headlong planning process in order to have something impressive to present to the venture committee in the final week of the lab.

As a result, the champions and the venture committee once again trashed the initiatives that the lab team members had worked so hard to come up with. This gave the lab a feeling of being doomed. What happened in practice was that we had set up a perfect opportunity for the champions to take back control of the lab. They took that opportunity with both hands. From being led by the lab team, the Alliance went through a painful inflection point where champions took over both ownership and control after three months of playing a peripheral, consultative role.

While this was upsetting at the time, it was far from a failure. The lab painfully reconfigured to align with the reality of power dynamics and went on to be successful.

During the weeks when we were at the office—a massive space donated and custom-renovated for us by Unilever in Navi Mumbai—we developed a pattern. The core team all lived in four apartments a short drive from the office. Initially we all had breakfast together and piled into two cars. We arrived at the office at least an hour before all the participants and had team meetings, reviewing aspects of the design and the schedule, before we formally started the day. After all the facilitating sessions, we returned to the library to debrief. Then we all piled back into the two cars to return to our apartments and have dinner together. The next day we did it all again.

In time, this pattern put a massive amount of strain on all of us. We were easily working twelve hours a day, sometimes longer if you factored in breakfast and dinner when we talked about the lab. My colleague, Joe McCarron, and I, who were sharing one of the apartments, decided to stop going to team breakfasts. Instead, we did yoga and ate breakfast on our own. In the evenings, we sometimes eschewed dinner with the team and, feeling slightly brain-dead, watched MTV instead. However, as the lab progressed, everyone got more and more tired.

It's hard to have perspective when you're exhausted. That was part of the challenge. We had inadvertently designed a brutal process, characterized by extreme power dynamics. Reflecting on this now, it seems obvious that the more pressure we put on ourselves, the more we fell back on an unreflective habitus, those ways of working that we were most used to.

The image that came to me when thinking about the lab was that of strapping a rocket to a car and lighting the fuse. A fuse had been lit underneath us, and we were burning jet fuel at a prodigious rate, zooming along this pre-plotted trajectory in a small, closed space. While in theory we could change the basic parameters of our journey, in practice we could not. Too many people were involved, too much money had been spent, and it had to get done—and of course the fuse had been lit and we were burning fuel.

FAIL EARLY, FAIL OFTEN

With the Bhavishya Lab, we had inadvertently set up an encounter that was heterogeneous and unequal. It brought together participants—maybe as many as half against their will—into an alien process, where huge demands were put on them. Among the participants themselves were huge differences in experience, in understanding, in status, and more. Many had never been asked to play such a strategic role before. Between the participants and the champions, yet another vast gulf of difference existed.

Despite all this, the lab produced far-reaching results (elaborated on in the next chapter) for a comparatively modest investment. A comment on an official evaluation read, "The Change

Lab is a giant step forward in the context of applying new social technology to produce radical changes in addressing a historical, social and mammoth issue of malnutrition in India. The teething problems would hopefully be overcome and several Change Labs will take the change process ahead."[4]

More often than not, there was a smell of burning tires in the air, as we traveled dizzyingly fast over terrain that was very rocky. Friction is a prerequisite for both movement and speed, as anyone who has tried driving a car over ice knows. Occasionally we'd hit a flat, smooth surface where we cruised for a while, but inevitably we would career into more difficult, crazy, cratered landscapes.

We never suffered a lack of friction from spinning our wheels or from *groupthink*, which is the situation that results from homogenous groups where everyone thinks the same. Almost every step we took was contested in some way. Someone was always trying to grab the wheel. Friction drove the lab at crazy speeds.

My colleague Adam wrote of the lab, "One of the members of the Alliance staff said to me two years later, 'The Champions said that they wanted us to achieve breakthrough innovations, but time and again they prevented us from deviating from the usual way of doing things. They were like the owners of an ocean-going boat that are not willing to let it get out of sight of the shore.'"[5]

Regardless of the many mistakes we made and all the things we would now do differently, the fact is that the Bhavishya Alliance went on for six more years and spun out many, many different innovative programs and initiatives. Our mistakes sometimes make it hard to acknowledge the good work that so many people did, the courage and the love that poured into trying to make the whole experience work. The smell of burning rubber, however, is still strong even six years later.

BUSINESS AS USUAL AND ITS RADICAL REFUSALS

The Generon Team left India just as the first monsoons were sweeping across Mumbai. The year before, almost a thousand people had drowned due to flooding. A flood warning went out as we were wrapping up the final debrief with the secretariat. We were advised to get to the airport as soon as possible; otherwise there was a real risk we would be trapped for days.

The drivers were worried because our route back to the apartments took us past the ocean, and the roads were at high risk from flash flooding. There was an air of panic. People were jumping into cars and speeding off. Gomathy got left behind, but she managed to get a cab. Part of the land in front of the building we were working in had collapsed due to the rains, which had now been falling for three days without pause.

An hour later, racing the floods, we were back at our apartments. We packed up all our belongings in twenty minutes, loaded back into the cars, and headed for a hotel right next to the airport. That final frenzied car ride through the rain-sodden streets of Navi Mumbai represented the end of our four-year Bhavishya adventure.

For much of my work during the Sustainable Food Lab, the Bhavishya Lab, and other labs, I took a highly critical, somewhat bad-tempered approach to what we were doing. I was in constant low-level struggles to change what I deemed to be problematic. Much of my time was spent in the weeds of details. Partly as a result of this and partly as a result of the organizational culture I was operating in, I emerged from four years of working with Generon exhausted. But strangely enough, I was more hopeful than ever. What was going on here?

After some pondering and stepping back from my experiences

with these first-generation social labs, I had a light-bulb explosion of an insight. *What was I being critical of?* The fact that I was being critical, that I was squabbling and fighting over details (and annoying a lot of people) meant something very important—there was actually something to improve upon, something worth fighting for—a foundation for a new way of addressing stuck social issues. Not only that, but the improvements I was imagining were clearly coming from some idea of what *could be*, that is, a vision for social labs.

The questions I left India with were very different from those I had when I left the Sustainable Food Lab. While exhausted, burned out, and disappointed, I took some comfort from the words of Anna Lowenhaupt Tsing: "Instead of starting with the dichotomy between global force and local response, these methods show the importance of contingent and botched encounters in shaping both business-as-usual and its radical refusals."[6]

5

The New Ecologies of Capital

The country needs and, unless I mistake its temper, the country demands bold, persistent experimentation. It is common sense to take a method and try it: If it fails, admit it frankly and try another. But above all, try something.

— Franklin D. Roosevelt

My experiences with the Food Lab and Bhavishya bracketed my work at Generon. One of the fallouts from Bhavishya was that Adam had started questioning the process. One of my mentors, Myrna Lewis, observed that this was undiscussable within Generon. The process, in other words, was sacrosanct in our culture and could not be doubted.

By late January 2007, it was clear that the two founding partners, Adam and Joseph, had irreconcilable differences on this issue. Joseph's point, to some extent, was simple but unmoving. He believed that the "interior conditions" were the core of the work and that if a small group of people held an intention strongly enough, it would happen. This "strange attractor" of intention would then attract others until there was a critical mass of people.

If one member of this small group did not believe that, then, well, it was impossible. Joseph believed this, and it was a matter of integrity for him. Adam, on the other hand, seemed to be holding this idea as a hypothesis—maybe it was true and maybe it wasn't.

The trouble in holding this position was its shadow side. Joseph was inadvertently making a judgment about Adam's interior conditions. He found Adam's lack of faith to be unacceptable because the work, to a large extent, required faith and, in particular, intentionality. Tom Rautenberg, half in jest and half seriously, referred to the situation as "Protestants versus Catholics."[1] And it actually felt like a deeply painful religious dispute. I was torn. I shared Joseph's beliefs, but I also instinctively felt that a diversity of beliefs was important.

During that time, I was supposed to produce a learning document on the Bhavishya experience. The experiences were so overwhelming that despite trying several times, I just couldn't figure out how to do it. I was on the verge of giving up when I talked to Mia Eisenstadt, a friend with a background in athropology. Mia has spent a lot of time working and living with communities in Thailand and South Africa with tough social issues and so, to some extent, was undeterred by the mess. She suggested that one way to proceed was for her to interview me. Her interview opened the floodgates to the beginning of unpacking and figuring out the lessons from the Bhavishya project. Together we wrote a detailed learning document, called "The Birth of the Bhavishya Alliance" that helped me process many of the issues relating to the lab and helped us envision what could be more effective in new labs.

Finally, a number of people were encouraging me to think about setting up something new, a firm that would be a clean break from the experiences of Generon. I kept putting it off. Then one day I asked Mia, should we do it? She said yes, we should.

THE END OF THE BEGINNING

On February 27, 2007, I sent out an email to the entire Generon team and a small number of friends, inviting them to a conversation about setting up a new organization. Out of this initial group, eight people stepped forward: three partners from Generon, Adam, Joe McCarron, and LeAnne Grillo; three of the founders of Pioneers of Change, Mille, Marianne, and Colleen (whom I had worked with for years prior to Generon); and my friends Jeff Barnum and Mia.

The end of Generon represented the end of a critical phase of work, that of conceptualizing and launching the first generation of social labs. The second phase of the work for me would take place within the context of a new organization, Reos Partners.

Forming Reos prompted me into a renewed exploration on the potential of social labs. In thinking about what we had done, I asked myself the question, what results do social labs actually produce?

In our original description of the Bhavishya Lab, we described the lab as cocreating three sets of results:

Initiatives: Three to six systemic, scalable, sustainable initiatives that can, by the end of 2007, reduce by 80 percent the number of children suffering from moderate or severe malnutrition in the five hardest-hit districts of Maharashtra.

Relationships: High-trust relationships among participating leaders and their organizations that will enable them to continue to develop and implement breakthrough solutions to this and other vital societal problems.

Capacities: Strengthened capacity of participating individuals and teams to undertake such deep innovation and change in large and complex organizational and societal systems.

The Bhavishya Alliance ran from 2006 till 2012. Including the three years of hard work to set up, it was a decade-long experiment. During this period, an extraordinary range of activities was undertaken. In April 2012, the Synergos Institute released a report on the legacy of the Alliance.[2]

The Taj Group of Hotels partnered with the Indian government to deliver a food diversification program. This involved ninety master trainers delivering training to 12,000 local women in one district alone. *Anganwadi* workers, self-help groups, and mothers' committees received training and mentoring to prepare meals.[3] The number of children benefiting from supplementary nutrition rose from 132,000 to over 149,000 in one month.

In another initiative, 7,800 girls completed a program designed to empower them by developing life skills. The program, called Girls Gaining Ground, increased their awareness of a broad range of issues, especially those relating to reproductive health and nutrition, and equipped them with vocational skills.

The lab had identified urban communities that suffered malnutrition as particularly vulnerable, especially when they lived in informal settlements, such as slums. The Day Care Centre's Initiative extended child-care services to the children whose mothers were working. Over a thousand children benefited from this service, with acute cases of malnutrition dropping significantly.

Finally, I was pleased to see results from an initiative focusing on information. The Computer-Aided Adult Literacy, Health and Nutrition Awareness Project (CAALP) provided training to over 1,260 women who participated in the project over a one-year period at ten locations. This had been one of the original ideas coming from the lab team.

The overall nutrition situation in Maharashtra improved during the period that Bhavishya ran. UNICEF, one of the co-conveners on the lab recently reported: "The preliminary findings of the survey indicate that the prevalence of stunting in children under-two decreased from 39.0% in 2006 to 22.8% in 2012. Importantly, prevalence of severe stunting in children under-two decreased from 14.6% in 2006 to 7.8% in 2012. This positive trend is seen both in rural and urban areas."[4] These statistics include many districts where the lab was operating.

EMERGING FORMS OF CAPITAL
AND PREVENTING COLLAPSE

Through examining these types of results we can see a particular class of outcomes emerging from each lab. They are best understood as different forms of *capital*. The first results we sought to cocreate with the labs were what we called *prototypes* or *initiatives*. When implemented, these provided a new set of services to stakeholders on the ground and are new forms of *physical capital* (infrastructure). The second set of results we sought to create, relationships, were a form of *social capital*. The third set of results, capacities, were a form of *human capital*. Finally, all the experience and formal lessons from both designing and implementing these labs were a form of *intellectual capital*.

The production of these different forms of capital contributes directly to preventing the collapse of social systems. John Michael Greer, in a paper entitled *How Civilizations Fall: A Theory of Catabolic Collapse,* outlines a theory that civilizations collapse because the productive capacities of a civilization fail "to meet maintenance requirements for existing capital."[5]

An analogy helps illustrate what Greer means. Imagine a farmer growing enough food every season to feed his or her family. If crop yields decrease each season, the farmer is forced to draw on grain stores. Eventually the stored grain will run out. Unless crop yields go up, the farmer will end up with no stock until there is nothing to feed the family. This is when bodies will start to break down their fat stocks in order to produce energy. Eventually, there will not be enough energy left in the field or in the body to sustain life.

Greer defines capital as including "physical capital such as food, fields, tools, and buildings; human capital such as laborers and scientists; social capital such as social hierarchies and economic systems; and information capital such as technical knowledge."[6]

Greer argues that civilizations collapse due to the depletion of natural resources, which causes a cycle of contraction where most capital stocks in a society are converted to waste. Human civilization is built on our ability to generate multiple forms of productive capital, which serves to meet societal needs for a period, before being converted to waste.

If, however, a civilization does not produce enough capital, then it starts consuming any capital stocks it possesses—just like a farmer with a failed crop and a family to feed. When the rate of waste being produced outstrips the rate of capital being produced—also known as the rate of consumption—then civilizations head toward ecological breakdown (what Greer calls *catabolic collapse*).

The divergent coupled trends described earlier in the example of Yemen—specifically, declining natural capital and increasing demand—paint a picture of catabolic collapse. This can be potentially averted if we produce enough capital, increase the efficiency of our capital consumption, or slow down the rate by which capital stocks are consumed.

An example of this is to ride a bicycle instead of drive. A bicycle is almost 800 times more efficient than the average car. It makes use of energy more effectively and produces less waste than a car. Driving uses more capital stocks and converts them to waste many times faster than cycling. Similarly, eating grain as opposed to meat is a more efficient use of capital stocks because it uses less water and less land in order to provide us with calories.

Why, however, is it that we drive cars or eat meat? The best way to understand these behaviors is to go back to the idea of habitus. The idea of habitus is deeper than the word *habit*. Bourdieu portrays a behavior that is deeply ingrained, mentally, physically, and systemically, one that is more of an addiction than a simple habit we can shrug off or just decide not to do. He writes that habitus exists "without being in any way the product of obedience to rules" and "can be collectively orchestrated without being the product of an organizing action of a conductor."

Finally, we're talking about "systems of durable, transposable dispositions." In other words, it isn't simply individual choice that we drive or eat meat; it's also because there are systemic pressures on us to make these choices. You risk getting run over if you cycle, or there are no meatless options on the menu. These structural features condition us to a set of responses. Habitus thus represents a set of "permanent dispositions." This permanence makes habitus "something like a property, a *capital*" (italics in original).

Breaking out of a cycle of collapse requires multiple stocks of capital. In addition to financial capital, we also need human capital, social capital, natural capital, and physical capital. We can create the option of strategically deploying these types of capital where we can actively produce them.

Bourdieu, in his explorations of habitus, makes the case for reclaiming the notion of capital from the economic and monetary spheres: "It is impossible to account for the structure and function of the social world unless one reintroduces capital in all its forms and not solely in one form recognized in economic theory."

Greer's description of catabolic collapse provides us with the backdrop against which we're working and articulates the challenge we're facing in broad civilizational terms. The paradox is that taking advantage of strategic opportunities requires us to deploy wisely what capital stocks we still possess in order to ensure that they generate new forms of capital.

Ultimately, we have to recognize that we are heading toward collapse because of habitus, which is nothing more than a decision about how we use energy, or our natural capital. Bourdieu explains, "Capital can be understood as the 'energy' that drives the development of a field through time." While we tend to see energy locked in a barrel of crude as distinctly different from the symbolic capital of culture, they are forms of energy represented in different forms of capital. At the core of our challenge is energy in the most holistic sense, and reconciling the sacredness and profanity of energy is the circle we must learn to square.

If our strategies—whether they are social laboratories or other approaches—are to precipitate systemic change (as distinct from reinforcing BAU), this requires that we enhance "the art of estimating and seizing chances." Producing these forms of capital improves our ability to *actually* take advantage of opportunities to change systems in the real world, a world in which plural forms of capital are shrinking.

Changing complex social systems requires that actors have competencies (human capital), the knowledge and understanding of what is to be changed (intellectual capital), the infrastructure and services required to deliver services (physical capital), the ability to pay for whatever is needed in order to do their work (financial capital), and the networks to organize themselves (social capital).[7]

In other words, we have to deploy capital to allow diverse stakeholders to find the opportunities latent in all crises.

THE DUMBEST IDEA IN THE WORLD

Success in a market-driven system has conventionally been measured in single forms of capital, or "mono" capital. How much money does a firm make? What financial returns does it provide to its shareholders? This notion of value, however, has taken a real beating in recent years. In a *Forbes* article, Jack Welch, the legendary CEO of General Motors, called the idea of maximizing shareholder returns as "the dumbest idea in the world."[8]

During the dot-com boom, I saw firsthand the extremely messy process by which innovation is actually supported. Private-sector innovation is funded from a variety of sources. Investors make their decisions based on *one key factor* and *one hunch*. The one key factor is their faith in the entrepreneur or the team behind a start-up. The one hunch is their guess as to the probability that an idea might fly and become a market leader. Yes, investors want to invest in start-ups that will make billions of dollars, but they know that this cannot be predicted with any confidence. If an investor sees an experienced team and has confidence in the vision articulated by those behind the start-up, they will take a risk and fork out the cash.

The venture capital strategy for dealing with the real risk of failure is to spread bet, as discussed earlier. The strength and the weakness of the sector come from the fact that investment decisions are made on the basis of faith in people. Sometimes this faith is misplaced, and sometimes it is not. Either way, no one keeps start-ups artificially alive because they don't want to tell their investors or look bad.

In the development sector, the notion of spread betting is unheard of. Instead, the rule of thumb is to *avoid failure*, which in practice means to avoid *admitting* failure, as failure in complex systems is unavoidable. Innovation is not an efficient process—it's messy.

When contrasted with other sectors, such as the for-profit sector or research more broadly, donors attempt to hold NGOs to a series of impossible standards, ensuring limited impact.[9] In his TED talk on all the things wrong with the "charity" sector (nonprofit), Dan Pallotta makes the point, "Our generation does not want its epitaph to read, 'We kept charity overhead low.' We want it to read that we changed the world."[10]

So how do we change the world? And what does that progress look like?

In an op-ed piece for the *New York Times*, Peter Buffett wrote:

> Money should be spent trying out concepts that shatter current structures and systems that have turned much of the world into one vast market. Is progress really Wi-Fi on every street corner? No. It's when no 13-year-old girl on the planet gets sold for sex. But as long as most folks are patting themselves on the back for charitable acts, we've got a perpetual poverty machine.[11]

Donors also seem to believe that people working on social issues should be able to predict the future. Numbers that do so are fiction. Some are better fictions than others, in that they are believable, but they are still fiction. Donors should note that investor confidence comes from experienced teams, the quality of their vision in addressing a need, and their ability to ship a product or deliver a service.

While the idea of market-driven approaches to social challenges sounds simple, obvious even, it gives rise to a whole host of problems. The micro-loan is the poster child often cited as an example of how market-approaches can help alleviate poverty. However, recent studies show that micro-loans create a whole new class of debtors locked into "micro-enterprises," unable to grow.[12]

Critics of central planning, such as Fredrick Hayek have argued that we need to let the market make decisions, but this replaces one set of problems with an entirely different and equally complex set of problems. It results in a shift from a horizontal, state-driven, planning approach to a vertical, market-driven, planning approach, as we see happening in the developmental and humanitarian spheres.

Organizations that focus all their efforts on the production of one form of capital, say financial, tend to be depleting other forms of capital at the same time. For example, strip mining depletes natural capital in order to generate financial capital, which is becoming less acceptable. It's also increasingly unnecessary because we can design approaches that produce multiple forms of capital. Organizations designed to produce only one form of capital are a dying breed.

The opportunity for next-generation labs is to take a more conscious approach to the production of new forms of capital. The challenge becomes one of ensuring that we do not fall into the habitus of BAU, producing single types of capital (i.e., financial) that do little more than further entrench BAU.

By reclaiming the production of multiple forms of capital from the economic and monetary spheres, instead of locking capital in *enclosures* (benefitting a small class of people), we can inject it into the commons in a virtuous cycle of healthy growth. Increasing the availability of multiple forms of capital in the commons provides one vision for what the non-profit world (the development and humanitarian spheres) could be focusing on.[13]

Nicholas Negroponte, the founder of the Media Lab at MIT, explains, "Some things will not happen in an economy only driven by markets. And that is the reason you need a Media Lab." He goes on further to say, "The lab was filled with solutions without knowing the problems. Seriously. We were not solving problems but inventing solutions and developing technology, in many cases for its own sake. Like a gold mine, companies just had to find it."

MORE RAINFORESTS, FEWER PLANTATIONS

How do we build environments that support innovation? One of the most successful ecologies for innovation is Silicon Valley. Venture capitalists and entrepreneurs Victor W. Hwang and Greg Horowitt set out to answer these questions: *What makes a place like Silicon Valley tick?* and *Can we replicate that magic in other places?*

In doing so, they created a model for innovation ecosystems called the Rainforest, which "nurtures budding ideas so they can grow into flourishing and sustainable enterprises." They explain, "The Rainforest model is more than a metaphor. Innovation ecosystems are not merely like biological systems; they are biological systems. . . . Human systems become more productive the faster that the key ingredients of innovation—talent, ideas, and capital—are allowed to flow throughout the system."[14]

Just as healthy rainforests are rich environments, teeming with life, so too are healthy social labs, cultivating diverse forms of capital. The rules for fostering healthy biological environments such as rainforests are very different from those for a planned plantation.[15]

By examining the first-generation social labs, we see that some produced new capital, not due to clear and conscious design but as by-products of our processes and intuition. So in some cases, we genuinely created new forms of capital, and in others, we fell into habitus and consumed capital. By reflecting carefully on these results, we can learn how to be more conscious of what we're try-ing to produce and then cultivate the conditions for that produc-tion. *More rainforests, fewer plantations.* If we can achieve this, then social labs have the potential to become engines that generate enormous amounts of capital in a world running dangerously low.

6

The Rise of the Agilistas

Sometimes at Edwards they used to play the tapes of pilots going into the final dive, the one that killed them, and the man would be . . . screaming into the microphone, but not for Mother or for God or the nameless spirit of Ahor, but for one last hopeless crumb of information about the loop: "I've tried A! I've tried B! I've tried C! I've tried D! Tell me what else I can try!" And then that truly spooky click on the machine. *What do I do next?*

— Tom Wolfe, *The Right Stuff*

In reflecting on the labs we ran, it became clear that first-generation social labs suffered a serious challenge. We called this the challenge of the *right-hand side*, which referred to the right-hand side of the U Process, concerned with realizing or cocreating. The right-hand side was all about action and in some ways the most familiar part of the work we did, and hence, most prone to habitus. Moving into action required the skills of crystallizing ideas and then prototyping. Beyond that, however, things got rather murky. While prototyping as an activity made sense, what did a *prototype* actually look like? Where does one take prototypes? What do you do with a successful prototype?

Looking at what worked during the Bhavishya Lab, I came to the conclusion that our design for it had followed an innovation process only up to a point, beyond which we fell back into a traditional planning mode—packaging up the initiatives that emerged from the lab into project proposals, staffing models, and Gantt charts. Habitus reasserted itself, partially because we ran out of theory to guide us as the pressure grew.

The approach we fell back on comes from a classic project management model, the Waterfall, which comes from software development and sees progress as a sequential movement, from top to bottom. Like all planning approaches it is built on the principle of BDUF (Big Design Up Front). But this expression of the planning paradigm has a terminal problem: it assumes perfect knowledge of the future.

Tom Rautenberg pointed out in one of his memos, "It's not clear to me who here is capable of executing successfully on the ideas and plans presented in these initiatives. Asking for volunteers with the time and passion to work on these projects as full-time initiative leaders is a scary recruitment process. *Where's the task-based competency model?* Where's the due diligence? Is anyone willing to reach out and find the most qualified professionals and/or organizations to lead these initiatives?" (italics added).

Bhavishya, however, retained its innovative approach despite the reassertion of habitus, largely by accident. Tex and the champions threw out the BDUF that the lab team presented to them because they weren't convinced *and* it was politically acceptable in the Indian context to allow this kind of failure. The lab team was not "too big to fail." In the end Bhavishya exemplified a prototyping approach.

After "failing" the lab team work and considering the next steps, the champions did not throw everything away. For example, the insight that we should intervene in the urban context—which had been ignored for a long time due to the complexities of informal settlements—resulted in a whole series of successful interventions. And so did the idea of using technology to address malnutrition.

After hewing to our approach so religiously, the fact that we resorted to BAU planning bothered me intensely. During the preparation phase of the lab, we had discussed how prototypes and initiatives would be managed. The main proposal on the table was to invite one of the Big Five consulting companies to come in and run a classic program-management process. I objected, citing a few instances where they had performed disastrously in the social sphere, but I couldn't put forward a coherent alternative at the time.

How is it that after all the hard work we had done, we were resorting to Soviet-era modes of command and control? Is this really the best we could do? What practices were out there that could help?

These questions set me along the path of trying to figure out what worked about the labs, what didn't, and why. What are they actually doing differently? Why did the Food Lab, the Bhavishya Lab, and, more broadly, social labs work?

THE PRACTICAL WISDOM OF SOCIAL LABS

In considering what parts of first-generation labs worked and what parts didn't, I applied three rules for evaluating effective practice.

Rule #1: Make what works stronger

Rule #2: Let go of what doesn't work

Rule #3: Discover what you don't have

We have a bias toward what's new, believing that new situations require new solutions. And we have a tendency of rejecting all past wisdom, which sometimes means throwing out what works alongside what doesn't. Applying these three rules of thumb to our practice gives us a more nuanced view of what effective practice looks like.

In order to better understand which practices fall under the first rule, I turned to a distinction first posed by Aristotle and later revised by Danish professor Bent Flyvbjerg.[1] In *The Nicomachean Ethics,* Aristotle makes the distinction between three chief intellectual virtues, including scientific knowledge, art, and practical wisdom, which he names *episteme, techne,* and *phronesis.*[2] Roughly, episteme is theory, techne is technology, and phronesis does not have a modern equivalent, but is perhaps the most relevant.

Aristotle begins his discourse on practical wisdom by observing, "The origin of action—its efficient, not its final cause—is choice, and that of choice is desire and reasoning with a view to an end."[3] During the course of his explanation of practical wisdom, Aristotle makes many distinctions of what practical wisdom is and isn't, the main one being the idea that practical wisdom is embodied; it is something that an individual actually does, "that which is *done.*"

Practical wisdom cannot be something that is done *to* other people, as many policy-oriented approaches do. Policy formulation and decisions of state are thus of a different nature than phronesis.

Surgeon Atul Gawande in his book, *The Checklist Manifesto: How to Get Things Right,* provides us with a study of the utility of phronesis-based approaches. Gawande draws on examples from fields as diverse as medicine, skyscraper design, and commercial flying. Gawande writes, "Under conditions of true complexity—

where the knowledge required exceeds that of any individual and unpredictability reigns—efforts to dictate every step from the center will fail."[4]

He argues that the humble checklist is an antidote to extreme complexity: "Checklists supply a set of checks to ensure the stupid but critical stuff is not overlooked, and they supply another set of checks to ensure people talk and coordinate and accept responsibility while nonetheless being left the power to manage the nuances and unpredictabilities the best they know how."[5]

Gawande illustrates how phronesis works in the face of complexity. It operates by developing and then providing us with a set of heuristics—codified rules, or checklists—based on experience, which help us make decisions in highly complex situations.

Perception of the particular, as opposed to the universal, is a major distinction between practical wisdom and what we could consider natural science. It requires an especially disciplined approach that is somewhat alien to the social spheres (but not to social sciences), where typically the starting point is advocating for a Utopian vision.[6]

STARTING WITH CURRENT REALITIES

One of the most important distinctions made in all the work we have done is to recognize the gap between what *is* and what we *desire*. In other words, our starting point was not what reality we as lab participants desired. Our starting point was trying to discern the realities as they existed for the people that the project aimed to help. Even when considering the future, the starting point is to consider what is plausible before getting into what is desirable.

In modern philosophical terms, this perception of the particular is known as phenomenology, from the Greek *phainomenon*, "that which appears." Founded in the early twentieth century by Edmund Husserl as a way of studying subjective experience, phenomenology developed multiple strands of thought.

A key philosophical challenge that arose from phenomenological approaches was the distinction between the subjective and the objective. Or, to get to the punch line, where does the world we perceive arise from?

A student of Edmund Husserl's, Martin Heidegger, in his most famous book, *Being and Time,* attempted to reconcile the dualism of subjectivity and objectivity through the notion of *Dasein,* a German word that means *being here* and is sometimes interpreted to mean *presence.*[7] Heidegger argued that the nature of the world is non-dualistic and that it does not make any sense to say that the subjective perceives the objective world; rather, *the two are the same.* (This is the origin behind the word *presencing* as used in the U Process.)

For our purposes, complex social problems present a particular challenge, which is, given their nature, how does one actually perceive the challenge in order to grasp and understand it? What does the "global financial crisis" actually look like? How does one perceive "climate change"? This becomes especially difficult if we accept principles of non-duality that mean we are not cleanly separate from these problems.

EVENTS RUPTURE DISPOSITIONS

To recap, the nature of complex adaptive systems is that their properties are emergent (arising from the interaction of parts), and these emergent properties are distinct from the properties of the parts (e.g., the wetness of the water is distinct from the properties

of hydrogen and oxygen). So how do we see the emergent properties of the whole?

Systems thinking as a discipline approaches complexity by
dealing with systems as *wholes* and not parts. This is accom-
plished through systems maps and heuristics, such as the Iceberg
Model, which makes a distinction between events, patterns, and
structures.[8]

In the Iceberg Model, what gives rise to patterns are structures
that are largely invisible to us, "below the waterline," where the
greatest mass of the iceberg is found. In this context, a structure
is more than physical; it is the product of a paradigm or mindset.
The Iceberg Model assumes that the most effective intervention
considers the whole system, or structure, as opposed to focusing
on, for instance, the event level. The assumption is that an event
is normalized, which, when repeated, gives rise to patterns, or
trends. Each event by itself is therefore insignificant and unwor-
thy of attention. Responding to events is the equivalent of dealing with symptoms rather than the causes; in other words, this
approach is non-systemic.

A phenomenological approach sees the same hierarchy of
events, patterns, and structures very differently. What we see
time and time again in the world are events that are unpredictable, what Nicholas Naseem Taleb calls "black swan" events.[9]
These events can result in vast changes to patterns, structures,
and our mental models. Recent examples of this include 9/11, the
unlikely election of Barack Obama, the global financial crisis,
and the Arab Spring.

History repeatedly testifies to the power of the singular event—
man lands on the moon or the fall of the Berlin Wall. The trouble,
of course, is knowing how to work in any meaningful way in the
present with what is ontologically unknown and fundamentally

new, something that does not presently exist but is emergent and may exist in the future?

The philosopher Alain Badiou addresses this gap in Heidegger's work in his book *Being and Event* and articulates a theory of such ontologically novel events.[10] He says, "I name 'event' a rupture in the normal disposition of bodies and normal ways of a particular situation. Or if you want, I name 'event' a rupture of the laws of the situation. So, in its very importance, an event is not the realization/variation of a possibility that resides inside the situation. *An event is the creation of a new possibility*"[11] (italics added).

Applying Badiou to the Iceberg Model turns it on its head. An *event*, in the Badioun sense, falls outside our ontology, outside of *being* (and hence of knowing). It is a black swan. And black swans are the forces that disrupt BAU. An unforeseen event results in changes—in how we think, in our practices, in our policies, and in the world, whether we like it or not. In other words, *events rupture dispositions.*

This, of course, is true not only of events experienced collectively but also individually. On the bus during one of the Food Lab learning journeys, an executive from a food transportation company got into a debate with an activist about climate change. No one facilitated—it was just the two of them. Later on, the executive credited this event with a shift in his position on climate change. In this way, the lab served as a site for an event. Simply by putting diverse people together, the probability of such encounters increases.

As individuals, we mark out our lives through events in the Badioun sense—when we move out of our parents' home, when we get married, when we first hold our children, and so on. Each of these events is special at the level of "possibility of possibility." The unfortunate and the unexpected equally mark our lives; an accident, an illness, or a death also signals disruption and new possibilities, ones that we may not want.

Nassim Nicholas Taleb points out, "The world in which we live has an increasing number of feedback loops, causing events to be the cause of more events (say, people buy a book because other people bought it), thus generating snowballs and arbitrary and unpredictable planet-wide winner-take-all effects."[12]

Innovation is a black swan. All sorts of people, from artists to technologists to researchers, grapple with ideas that are new all the time without worrying about the kinds of problems that Heidegger or Badiou brought attention to. Practitioners, in other words, have no real problem imagining things that don't exist. In practice this is what innovation, from its root *novus*, or new, is all about.

The general sense that inventors and artists are slightly crazy comes from the fact that they deal in things that don't exist for the rest of us. There is a mysterious aspect to the act of creation. Imagine the first time Gustav Eiffel, who conceived of the Eiffel Tower, told people about the idea. How did they react to the idea of a tower made of steel bigger than anything ever seen before? How does one prove that this is the right thing to do? Imagine if they had said, "Can you prove to me this makes sense?"

This is Badiou's point—that events fall outside of what currently exists and hence outside of conventional modes of knowing. There is no proving them; there is only doing them and learning from this doing. If we internalize this idea, it has profound implications about how we think about and attempt change in the world.

In all this, Heidegger is pointing out that the objective and the subjective are inseparable—there is no "outside." Everything is "inside." This insight, on the non-dual nature of *being*, is the philosophical backstory to the theory of action presented here, a theory of how to intervene in the world with all its complexity and messiness.

Philosophically, the Heideggerian position is that we are the systems we wish to change, and the systems we wish to change are inseparable from us. Admittedly, this is a very difficult request to make of people, particularly those of us who are classically trained to believe in objectivity and scientific neutrality. Our usual response to challenges that are too hard to grasp whole is to separate them into manageable problems or parts.

This idea of *presence* is a key part of the U process. Presence is a way in which the self and the other become the same. Heidegger saw presence as resolving the dualism of subjective and objective, and drew on the notion of Dasein. According to Heidegger, the route to ontology (the nature of existence) is through radical phenomenology. That is, if it is rigorous enough, phenomenology will allow us to understand the nature of reality. Badiou builds on Heidegger by saying that ontology does not cover everything because there are also events, which includes moments of insight as well as those moments when the world experiences something new. These events give rise to new systems, structures, and realities.

Badiou makes the radical point that these ruptures that result in a recasting of truth *come prior to their verification.* In other words, we cannot generate new systems, new structures, and new realities that are verifiable prior to their coming into being.[13]

The Bhavishya Lab, to take one example, was an event in this sense but it was also a site for events. And it succeeded in its disruptive goal. If Badiou calls a rupture with the present an event, then social labs are an attempt to create an event that introduces to participants the possibility of something ontologically new. A way of provoking a rupture, a new system in which children are not malnourished, a world where our resources challenges are better managed and so on—this is how I understand social innovation.

We have to keep reminding ourselves that such outcomes *cannot be theoretically falsifiable in advance*. We cannot, in other words, know what new solutions to problems and challenges are before they are created, discovered, or invented; otherwise we would have implemented them already.

Where we demand certainty, or falsifiable theory, before we act, we are essentially asking for an elimination of risk and failure. It's a bit like asking for a guarantee of a great insight, a great discovery, or a great piece of art. As far as being innovative is concerned, this is impossible. When we examine how scientific and technological development proceed, we see that this is a well-known fact. It's the difference between buying a great work of art versus supporting the development of a great artist. The genius of Silicon Valley is in recognizing this insight and building an ecology that increases the probability that a start-up will succeed.

When we loaded participants into buses and trains and sent them to observe the phenomenon of child malnutrition and when we asked participants to eat what the families of the malnourished were eating, we were embarking on acts of perception. In mapping out systems and attempting to grapple, however crudely, with the whole system, we were trying to understand the processes by which child malnutrition was constructed and, hence, how it could be deconstructed.

All of these actions rest philosophically, on the practical wisdom and the practical philosophy of Aristotle, Heidegger, Badiou, and their contemporary commentators. In contrast, BAU strategies are primarily rooted in episteme and techne. The overlap between these two types of intellectual virtues gives rise to the modernist planning paradigm and technocrat strategies. The horrors of modernist technocratic paradigms missing phronesis are marvels of science and engineering. My bafflement fifteen years ago when I left the university was at how modern physics was taught. Why were we not being taught the practical wisdom required to wield the products of episteme and techne? It seemed to me that physicists needed to understand the profoundly social implications of their science, such as the nuclear bomb. This would require a degree of practical knowledge or wisdom that went beyond the physics laboratory. But this had no place in how we were taught.

The promise of a partnership among the realms of techne, episteme, and phronesis is the promise of a partnership of diverse intellectual virtues that together represent the best of humanity. Now, perhaps more than any period in human history, we have a profound need for what Aristotle called *phronimos*, the person of practical wisdom.

What I witnessed and learned throughout the last decade is phronesis. All the teachers I worked with—Myrna Lewis, Adam Kahane, LeAnne Grillo, Joseph Jaworski, Otto Scharmer, Matt Gelbwaks, Grady McGonagill, and many others—are phronimos, people of practical wisdom.

The nature of complex social challenges means that entire teams of phronimos are required to grasp a situation and make decisions about what to do in situations of great complexity.

THE RIGHT STUFF

It took only three years to act on Rule #3 (discover what you don't have) in answer to Tom's question, "Where's the task-based competency model?" Then it took another three years of practice to figure out how to make it work within the context of social labs.

The approach is called *Scrum*, and it is built on top of a software development philosophy called *Agile*. Scrum and Agile are textbook examples of phronesis. They are vastly superior to the neo-Soviet, command-and-control, waterfall project-management approach so common today.

In his study *Unlearning Project Management*, David A. Schmaltz writes, "Koskela and Howell observe that most project work is more like a scientific experiment than a finely determinable set of performance criteria. In scientific experiments, we progress even when our experiment fails, not only when it succeeds. Our plans are frequently hypothetical, intended to guide value creation, not simply blueprints guiding assembly."[14]

In early 2001, seventeen "independently minded practitioners" came together and penned "The Manifesto for Agile Software Development." The Agile manifesto is a call to arms against Big Design Up Front, and it represents a genuinely radical break in how software is developed. It articulates four values:

Individuals and interactions over processes and tools

Working software over comprehensive documentation

Customer collaboration over contract negotiation

Responding to change over following a plan

Scrum was developed on top of these values. The basic ideas that constitute Scrum are startling in both their simplicity and audacity.

Teams work together at the start of a project to articulate a success scenario. Once this scenario is articulated, the team brainstorms a list of all the tasks they need to complete in order to achieve success. This list is called the *backlog*.

Then teams are organized into cycles, composed of twenty-four-hour periods and longer lengths of time, say, a week or two, called *sprints*. (Sprint lengths can vary.) On the first day of a sprint, the team decides which tasks from the backlog it will attempt to complete during that sprint, which might be a week or perhaps two.

Once this is decided, the team *scrums* (basically huddles) every twenty-four hours. They report back to each other what they are going to do in the next twenty-four hours and what they need help with. A coach then troubleshoots problems outside of this short meeting. A daily scrum might last just fifteen minutes.

Once a team completes at least one sprint, the weekly planning meetings include a *retrospective* of what was done the week before. The goal is for teams to sprint until they complete all their tasks, thus achieving the success scenario.

One of the radical parts of Scrum is that the backlog of tasks can change dynamically while a team is engaged in a sprint. These changes do not alter what the team does during a sprint. Rather, at the end of the sprint, the team goes to the backlog to see what to do in the next sprint.

Under the four values in the manifesto are twelve principles. Decisions for what tasks to undertake are guided by providing value to the customer on an ongoing basis, as laid out by the first principle: "Our highest priority is to satisfy the customer through early and continuous delivery of valuable software." The second principle is "Welcome changing requirements, even late in development. Agile processes harness change for the customer's competitive advantage."

In Scrum, successful teams learn to establish what is called a *stable velocity*, where velocity represents the amount of work a team is able to complete during a sprint. This leads to establishing a *sustainable pace*, or a realistic pace for delivering the work, based on one of the principles in the manifesto: "Agile processes promote sustainable development. The sponsors, developers, and users should be able to maintain a constant pace indefinitely."

Teams, in other words, focus on building working prototypes that actually add value in the here and now, as opposed to some time in the distant future. This is the approach that we tried to take in all of our first-generation social labs. The point of a prototype is to start to deliver results as soon as possible and, in the process of iterating, to improve. That is the difference between a pilot and a prototype.

Why are agile approaches so well suited to complex social challenges? The concept of an agile approach arose from practitioners trying to figure out a better way of developing software, which was getting exponentially more complex each day. The conditions under which this approach was developed are similar to the context in which we were developing prototypes.

BDUF, the waterfall, and traditional planning are all *fragile* approaches, in the sense that the more stress put onto a system, the more likely it is to buckle and break. The planning-based approach finds its highest political expression in the Soviet Union, an entity that lived and died by planning. As our context becomes more obviously complex, we will become increasingly aware that neo-Soviet approaches put us squarely on the road to collapse.

Agile development, on the other hand, represents an "anti-fragile" approach.[15] In the midst of uncertainty, change, and complexity, agile teams—if properly set up—get stronger. Their development muscles grow as teams practice and get better at internalizing agile processes and delivering value in multiple forms of capital. Finally, agile processes are all about timely responses to the unplanned event in order to create more value.

Agile, in other words, eats black swans for breakfast.

My introduction to Scrum and Agile came through agile

trainer Matt Gelbwaks. In early 2009 Matt and I initially spent a day together in our US offices, where we came up with a rough, back-of-the-envelope method for how to apply agile approaches to the right-hand side of the U Process.

Implementing the agile approach was not easy. This was partly because it represented such a quantum shift in culture, and no one—not us, our staff, or our clients—understood this new culture. Lab team members would constantly ask, "But what's the deadline?" and we would explain it the same way every time they asked: the end of the week if the task was on their list that week.

Agile development demands multiple shifts in perspective, ranging from how we work with clients to how we promise and deliver on results. To experienced project managers and clients, these shifts don't necessarily make sense when viewed individually. The other reason why this is difficult in practice is that it demands discipline. And this discipline is hard.

The difficulties were both external and internal. They were external in that we had to understand and master a different way of working with new processes and protocols, where it was not obvious what to do. The internal difficulties involved practices that did not make sense to us, which provoked emotional reactions and resistance.

Interestingly, the person who took to agile development the most quickly was Leo Eisenstadt, the youngest person on our team. Leo, in contrast to the rest of us, is a natural *agilista*. He has no emotional attachment to planning-based approaches. He does not care about how things have been done traditionally; he wants to know what works in the here and now.

If BAU approaches are akin to flying a plane on autopilot in a storm, then agile approaches are more like a test pilot flying a prototype plane into the heart of a storm. The test pilot actively pushes the plane beyond its known limits in order to gather information on how to improve its performance. In fact, this is where the expression "pushing the envelope" comes from, an *envelope* being an aeronautical term that describes the safest outer boundary for an aircraft.

In his 1979 account of the first astronauts, Tom Wolfe explores what makes someone want to sit on a rocket and wait for the fuse to be lit. Many of these first astronauts were experimental test pilots. In his exploration of the psychology of these pilots and what drove them, Wolfe coined the phrase that became the title of his book—*The Right Stuff.* When it comes to complex social challenges, agile provides us with a sense of "the right stuff" we need to be cultivating.

7

Steps Toward a Theory of Systemic Action

There is nothing so practical as a good theory.
— Kurt Lewin

When the first astronauts went through their paces in the high deserts around Edwards Air Force Base, they were reluctant instruments of what Heinrich Heine calls "men of thought." They were asked by the "white-coats" to do things that made little sense to them. From time to time they protested against being treated like experimental chimpanzees and pushed back. Ultimately, however, they made their grudging peace with the fact that they were subjects in a vast experiment based on theories they did not know.

Much of the BAU behavior is the product of theory, most of it long forgotten or remembered only by specialists. If we are to come up with effective responses to complex actions, we need to align our actions with our best thinking about complex social challenges. Theory must inform our actions. When we think that's not the case, it's usually because *invisible* theory is informing our actions. We therefore need to be aware of these underlying theories. At the moment, much is guided either by theory ill suited to complexity or what are sometimes labeled "theories of change," which are little more than elaborate hypotheses labeled as theory.

While what is being outlined here is being called *theory*, this needs a little clarification. As previously explained, practical wisdom is best expressed through heuristics (rules of thumb, checklists) that are highly context-dependent, as opposed to universal principles, which are independent of context. A theory rooted in phronesis is therefore more akin to a recipe or a checklist than to a normal science theory or even a social science theory.

A recipe or a checklist is predictive in the sense that if one combines certain ingredients under particular conditions and uses the prescribed techniques, one gets the expected outcome.[1] However, it does not make sense to think of either being *falsifiable* in the way we would think of theory in the natural sciences. A recipe that fails in the hands of a bad cook does not mean the recipe does not work. But then how does one tell if a recipe is bad? Well, one simple answer is experience. When you cook it, it tastes bad. If a recipe corresponds to a set of instructions for producing a particular outcome, then the point of phronesis is that the only real way of learning how to cook is to cook.

Just as handing a novice a recipe will not produce a world-class dish (other than in the same sense that enough monkeys bashing enough typewriters will produce a Shakespearean play), no amount of simply handing people maps or tools will produce systemic action. A single-minded focus on either episteme or techne is like buying the best cookbooks and top-of-the-line cookware without bothering to learn how to cook. It doesn't make much sense.

1ST REQUIREMENT: CONSTITUTE A DIVERSE TEAM

The recent focus on the imperative for business to innovate has resulted in a new slew of insights into how best to build teams that are good at innovation. In their book *X-Teams*, Deborah Ancona and Henrik Bresman make the case that building teams "that lead, innovate, and succeed," requires what they call *X-teams*, where X stands for *external*.[2]

They elaborate:

> The world is plagued by complex problems like poverty, global warming, and political violence. These problems can only be addressed when people from diverse sectors like business, government and nongovernmental organizations (NGOs) work together. It is teams that will ultimately be the major actors in carrying out this important work.[3]

X-teams differ from traditional teams in that they have "high levels of external activity," and they must "combine all that productive external activity with extreme execution inside the team."[4] Extreme execution is simply another way of saying that the team must focus not only on the external, but must be able to effectively combine external activity with the development of effective internal processes. Finally, X-teams "incorporate flexible phases, shifting their activities over the team's lifetime."[5] In other words, X-teams need to be agile in terms of their processes. Focusing on the external, as opposed to inside an organization, clues us into how to convene teams that are good at innovating.

Given the opportunity to bring together a dream team to work on a systemic challenge, who would you pick, and how would you pick them?

On the first-generation social labs we ran, the rule of thumb for answering this question was "diverse and influential." There are two components to this rule of thumb that bear examination and explanation. *Diverse* was interpreted to mean *multi-sector,* which in turn was interpreted to mean that we constituted teams with representatives from government, civil society, and the business sectors.

The second half of the rule of thumb—influential—raises the question: who in the first half of the twenty-first century is influential?

The Half-Life of Power

> Power is decaying.
>
> — Moises Naim

In 1956 the sociologist C. Wright Mills wrote a book called *The Power Elite.*[6] The premise of the book was that the leaders of the military, corporate, and political spheres of society held power and that ordinary citizens were comparatively powerless. Mills's conception of power was relatively traditional—a small elite leadership has the most influence on society.

The convening strategy we deployed in order to recruit "diverse but influential" participants for first-generation social labs was a classic Millsian approach. Captains of industry, government ministers, and the heads of large NGOs were deemed to be influential. Grassroots activists, artists, care workers, farmers, and members of rural communities, for example, were not deemed influential enough.

The French philosopher Michel Foucault revolutionized our understanding of power in the decades following Mills. Foucault showed through detailed historical analysis that the nature of power was very different from traditional conceptions of hard power, that is, as something that could be owned and used like an instrument. Power was instead symbolic and relational. He argued, "There is no power relation without the correlative constitution of a field of knowledge, nor any knowledge that does not presuppose and constitute at the same time power relations."[7]

In 1991 Joseph Nye from Harvard University coined the phrase "soft power," describing it as "the ability to get what you want through attraction rather than coercion or payments. It arises from the attractiveness of a country's culture, political ideals, and policies. When our policies are seen as legitimate in the eyes of others, our soft power is enhanced."[8]

Then, in the last ten years, the notion of who is influential and who is not has morphed several times. Bruce Sterling commented, "Wikileaks and Facebook—which weren't even around five years ago—have more political clout than the state department and the US military combined. It's nothing to clap about. It's actually a calamity."[9]

The rise of the networked society and increasing social complexity has prompted new research that has clarified our understanding of how highly connected societies function. In a 1998 *Nature* article, Duncan Watts and Steve Strogatz articulated a mathematical model for what they called "small-world networks."[10] Strogatz and Watts applied their model to a sociological explanation of how our world works. Their research explains what has been called "small-world phenomena" (such as the idea that we're all six degrees of separation away from actor Kevin Bacon), but also covers the rapid spread of viruses, the connectivity of the Internet, and gene networks.[11]

The basic idea is that small-world networks consist of clusters that are weakly linked through a small number of network agents. In social terms, this means that people are related to each other through relatively small, tight clusters, but a few members of these clusters are weakly connected to other clusters. It's through these weak links that information, viruses, and connections in general occur.

The rise of small-world networks and what are called *scale-free* networks (like the Internet) changes the notion of influence in society. Paul Adams, who previously led Google's social research team and is currently working at Facebook, counters what he calls "the myth of the 'influentials.'"[12] Adams argues, "Trying to find highly influential people is a risky strategy."[13] This is because the success of any highly connected individual fluctuates wildly, and it's not clear how we actually measure influence consistently.

During the first-generation social labs we ran, looking for influentials was our convening strategy. In the case of the Bhavishya Alliance, we spent millions of dollars and hundreds of hours interviewing people across India in an effort to find the right "diverse but influential" participants from the entire field of child malnutrition.

Commenting on Watts, Adams writes, "The most important factor was not whether there were influential people but whether there was a critical mass of easily influenced people who were connected to other people who were easy to influence. When this critical mass of connected people didn't exist, not even the most influential people could get an idea to spread widely."[14]

My colleague Mustafa Suleyman, in thinking about our convening strategy, had the breakthrough idea of simply broadcasting an invitation through our networks and seeing who turned up. After attempting our original strategy unsuccessfully while convening the Finance Innovation Lab (very few people from the finance sector we spoke to wanted to join an effort to change it), we eventually sent out an email invitation to five thousand targeted people. This resulted in running three events where three hundred people turned up. These people eventually coalesced into a network that formed the participants of the Finance Lab. It cost a fraction of what our Bhavishya convening strategy cost and took a month, compared to two years of searching high and low. This is what I refer to as *open convening*.

Interestingly, for the Finance Innovation Lab, this strategy yielded a group that is not influential in Millsian terms and has instead created more of an inside-out dynamic, where key mainstream actors in the financial sector were relatively wary of participating fully in this group. The question of what impact this group of hundreds of people will have on the financial system is still open and in play.

The question of how to constitute a dream team to respond to a complex social challenge therefore remains open. Developments such as the rise of the networked society, more sophisticated understandings of power, and the actual evidence base for who has influence in society means that people who would not be considered elite in Millsian terms are now able, more than in any other period in history, to determine the shape of their own lives.

This shift in how power is approached represents one of the most significant differences between first-generation social labs and next-generation labs.

2ND REQUIREMENT: DESIGN AN ITERATIVE PROCESS

Here's a thought experiment. Imagine that you're given a task, either by your boss, a client, or a minister. The task is to get a group of people who are standing in a valley to climb a mountain. You're free to use whatever means necessary in order to achieve this task, and the assumption is that people will stay on top of the mountain after they've been moved. What would you do?

Perhaps you simply ask people to go to the top of the mountain.

What would happen? The first thing that would happen is that people would ask you why you want them to go. Soon after that, at least one person would ask the feared question, "Who are *you* to tell us where to go?" What do you do then? Well, you need a strategy.

A bad strategy would be to simply describe the desired outcomes, without providing any information about how to achieve them.[15] A competent strategy would propose how to get the group from the valley to the top of the mountain, with a clear grasp of the practical difficulties and taking them into account. A planning-based approach would exhaustively document every step of the journey, logframe it, and then hire a bunch of people to execute it. The longer the journey, the more uncertain the terrain and the higher the probability that the group following a planning-based approach will fail.

A Statist or Civil Society strategy would consider a number of BAU options. A developmental strategy would involve convincing the group that it had to move for its own good, and it would probably take years. A humanitarian strategy might be to tell the group, to the dramatic backbeat of helicopter blades, that they are about to be swept away by a tsunami. A security strategy would involve riot police and vans that would forcibly move people at gunpoint. If a battle-space strategy is being used, the group is assumed to be hostile because all other strategies have been tried, and it's questionable how many of the group would survive the air war prior to the ground assault in order to be forced up the mountain.

In the last two instances, the solutions are unlikely to be easy or sustainable. It's likely that once the threat of force recedes, the group would simply steal back to the valley after dark. Or worse, they would return and lace the road with IEDs to deter further assaults. Of course, each of these approaches gets increasingly expensive, requiring more resources and resulting in more damage.

A market-oriented approach would be to wait until others had created a market for the journey. Or if a client were willing to take the risk and foot the bill, a marketing communications agency would design an advertising campaign to convince the group that it was cool to get to the top where winners lived like kings and that only losers lived in the valley. Then the task would be to set up a limo service to take those who could afford it to the top as quickly and painlessly as possible, while selling food, supplies, and equipment to those too poor to get the A-list treatment. And so on.

In base terms, what is required to get the group from the valley to the top of the mountain is energy. Gravity means that a certain amount of energy is required to move the mass of the group. This minimal energy must come from somewhere. If the group decides it's going to drive up the hill or take helicopters, then the amount of energy required goes up immensely. The most sustainable solution to the challenge is, of course, that people decide for themselves to get to the top of the mountain, collaborate with each other, and get there using their own locomotion—to walk up. This is a *subsistence* strategy and the only sustainable one. As a solution, it does not require a helping industry, a military-industrial complex, or an energy sector to drill the Arctic. And it doesn't produce industrial-scale environmental waste. At most, the requirements are food, water, and suitable clothes.

In other words, there are more and less effective strategies for getting the group from the valley to the mountaintop. Sometimes, the scale, complexity, and abstraction of our challenges blind us to the simple verities, such as "Behind the world's most difficult problems are people—groups of people who don't get along together. You can blame crime, war, drugs, greed, poverty, capitalism or the collective unconscious. The bottom line is that people cause our problems."[16]

What is certain, however, in all these scenarios, is that if the group does not want to move, it's difficult and expensive (in all senses of the word) to move it—with no guarantee that the group will stay *moved*. What's also certain is that if this group decided, *truly* decided, it was going to get to the top of the mountain, it would take a lot to stop them, as countless epic journeys and expeditions literally demonstrate.

The task of supporting this group to move of its own volition is typically what we, in our work, call *process facilitation* because it focuses on the process of a group self-determining where it wants to go and then inviting a facilitator to help it get there. The role of the facilitator then becomes to support the group and deal with the *how* of the journey, issues such as leadership (is anyone leading?), decision making, conflict resolution, and clarifying purpose (for when the journey gets really tough).

A good strategy in the context of complexity would include an iterative process. The simplest form of an iterative process is trial, error, observation, and reflection. You try something out, wait to see what happens, and then make another move based on what you've learned. The more complex the challenge, the more sophisticated a search strategy needs to be to find the way through the terrain, but the core essence of any iterative process is the same. Of course the ideal trial is one that is fail-safe—one that results in no lasting damage if it doesn't succeed.

The notion of a *process* is philosophically oriented toward *social constructivism*. The idea behind social constructivism is that *social* processes produce everything we usually assume as having an *essential* or objective character. Social constructivism arose out of a school of thought labeled the sociology of scientific knowledge (SSK) that studies science as a social activity. The more radical proponents of this school would argue that scientific or technological labs are also social labs, in that social processes constitute them and determine what happens in them.

3RD REQUIREMENT: ACTIVELY CREATE SYSTEMIC SPACES

Crane Stookey runs an experiential education program called the Nova Scotia Sea School. It is based on the Container Principle: the wisdom of no escape.

Stookey explains how this works:

> The image that best describes this principle is the stone polisher, the can that turns and tumbles the rocks we found at the beach until they turn into gems. The rocks don't get out until they're done, the friction between them, the chaos of their movement, is what polishes them, and in the end the process reveals their natural inherent brilliance. We don't paint colours on them, we trust what's there.[17]

The work then of process, in the context of the Sea School, is to create an environment—a container or a space—that lends itself to experiential learning. Social labs are space in the same sense. Process is used not in order to engineer a pre-determined set of outcomes, but rather, to create a container within which strategy can emerge from the friction of diverse participants working together as a team.

This notion is echoed by Steven Johnson in his book, *Where Good Ideas Come From*: "Some environments squelch new ideas; some environments seem to breed them effortlessly."[18]

John LeCarre once wrote, "The desk is a dangerous place from which to view the world." Yet, so many of our efforts to address complex challenges are born, live, and die at desks and boardroom tables. These spaces are by their nature homogenous and static, especially when contrasted with spaces that are actively produced and are dynamic, like the Sea School.

Static spaces are designed to support static organizational structures where relationships are carved into org charts, facts are written in stone, access is controlled, and people come to work and do the same thing day in and day out. The furniture is bolted down, the doors are shut, and the world is a computer screen. Such spaces are designed for control, Soviet in spirit, and dominated by a set of unchanging dispositions.

In practice, unless you're an architect, urban planner, or interior designer, you probably work in an inherited space, that is, a space over which you exercise very little active control. The world, in static space, is not something we actively construct. Perhaps we can pin some postcards to a wall or put photos on our desks, but that's largely the extent to which modern working space is actively shaped by those within it.

Henri Lefebvre attempts to articulate a "unitary theory" of physical, mental, and social space, which serves to diagnose our current condition.[19] For our purposes, Lefebvre makes three main claims. The first is "Social space is indistinguishable from mental space (as defined by philosophers and mathematicians) and physical space (as defined by practico-sensory activity)." The second is that social space is a social product. Third, "This act of creation is a process [and] . . . every social space is the outcome of a process with many aspects and many contributing currents, signifying and non-signifying, perceived and directly experienced, practical and theoretical."[20]

These three claims by Lefebvre can be used to understand how BAU habitus operates. BAU is the result of historical processes, which have produced a number of spaces. These BAU spaces—development, humanitarian, security, and battle spaces—can all be thought of as examples of what Bourdieu calls *fields,* or what Lefebvre calls *dominated space,* which are "invariably the realization of a master's project." All societies produce their spaces according to Lefebvre. BAU spaces are the products of a particular society—ours—that values episteme and techne over phronesis. Our spaces reflect this bias, and, hence, BAU spaces are hostile to the activities of phronesis.

We therefore require the production of a new, systemic space supportive of phronesis and of emergent strategy. Lefebvre comments, "A new space cannot be born (produced) unless it accentuates differences."[21] This space is in actuality a heterogeneous space, one that allows for the informal to exist with the formal. It's a space that's externally oriented but can also turn inward when the need arises, one that is supportive of diversity and difference.

Finally, it's clear from the countless examples of the kinds of spaces that engender creativity, innovation, and problem solving, that such spaces must be autonomous, allowing high degrees of freedom. Systemic action, therefore, requires a particular space to support it and a particular organizational form that is actively designed to be systemic in nature. This space is what I refer to as a *social laboratory.*

8

Starting a Social Lab: Seven How-Tos

Having a strategy suggests an ability to look up from the short term and the trivial to view the long term and the essential, to address causes rather than symptons.

— Lawrence Freedman, *Strategy: A History*

A social lab is a strategic approach toward addressing complex social challenges. As a strategy, it isn't too hard to grasp. It can be stated simply. Bring together a diverse, committed team and take an experimental, prototyping-based approach to addressing challenges systemically, that is, at a root-cause level. Keep going. That's it.

STRATEGIC VERSUS TACTICAL THINKING

A key challenge I have seen over the years with responses to complex social challenges comes when strategy is confused with tactics. What's the difference between strategy and tactics? According to Wikipedia, "In common vernacular, 'tactical' decisions are those made to achieve greatest immediate value and 'strategic' decisions are those made to achieve the greatest overall value irrespective of immediate return."[1]

Strategy is therefore concerned with the whole, while tactics are concerned with a part.

Addressing complex social challenges requires deep strategic commitment coupled with radical tactical flexibility. We are required by the nature of the challenge to take a long-term view, to make serious strategic commitments that survive short-term reversals of fortune. At the same time, we need to take an experimental approach, to try things out and hold them lightly. This combination of deep strategic commitment with tactical lightness is very hard to pull off because it simultaneously requires different temperaments.

In fact, dominant responses to complex social challenges often confuse what we need to hold fast to versus what we need to hold lightly. Our commitments should not be to tactics—to a particular plan or technique. Rather, we should reserve our deepest commitments for strategic goals.

I came across an example of such confusion after the collapse of the United Nations Framework Convention on Climate Change talks in Copenhagen. The climate movement was trying to figure out its next strategic move, and we were helping the Climate Action Network with its strategy. As part of this work, we did two things: we interviewed a wide range of stakeholders and we looked at what the science was saying.

In one interview with an individual from a leading climate NGO, we talked about what the science was demanding compared to the demands his NGO was publicly making. "Well, the science is saying that in order to avoid dangerous climate change we need to reduce Germany's emissions by 90 percent," he told me, "but if I say that in public, no one will take me seriously, so we say 60 percent." I played that back, "So you know that the figure of 60 percent is not right, yet you make a tactical decision not to talk to people about the real strategic target, which is more like 90 percent?" He looked at me glumly, "Yes, that's right."

One consequence of this decision was that I kept coming across signs of immense confusion in the public domain, where people believed that 60 percent was sufficient because a leading climate NGO was saying it, but then the scientists seemed to be saying something different. Who to believe? Of course this was a conscious tactical decision by one NGO, but the implication was widespread confusion between what the actual strategic goal was versus a tactical goal, picked for a short-term credibility gain.

There are, of course, many more day-to-day examples. Organizations suffer this problem all the time when they need to make a decision to pursue a short-term interest that's not core to their strategy for financial benefit. There are conscious ways of making a tactical decision. For example, we know our core mission is selling apples, but we're going to be selling bananas for a season because there's a killing to be made. Trouble arises when, after doing this a few times, you're losing huge amounts of money and no one remember what your core business is. Is it apples or bananas? Who knows? An endless stream of corporate giants have gone bust because they forgot what they were good at, got cocky, and over-diversified, lured by short-term tactical gains.

Strategy is a commitment to a wider course of action—to winning the World Cup, to ending Apartheid, to ending gun violence in our communities and so on—coupled with some sense of direction. Strategy is not pure intentionality. We want to end gun violence, and our best guess as to how to achieve it is through education. Or we want to address unemployment, and the direction we pick is helping people set up new social enterprises. Strategy, in this sense, is a commitment to action and then actual actions taken. Strategy is *not* sitting in a room coming up with a detailed plan and then instructing other people to implement that plan. That's planning.

Tactics, on the other hand, are simply ways of achieving strategic goals. The saying *there are many ways to skin a cat* refers to tactics. "I've tried A! I've tried B! I've tried C! I've tried D! Tell me what else I can try!" reflects tactical flexibility when confronted with complexity. An example of confusing strategy with tactics is the person who finds that skinning a cat is hard work and so decides to peel a banana instead. (I've tried A! I've tried B! They don't work! I'm going home!)

Being unable to tell the difference between a strategy and a tactic means we risk treating social labs as short-term tactics, which is a recipe for frustration because when we fail to get short-term results, we'll declare failure. A social lab is a strategy, requiring strategic commitment. Treating social labs as another tactic, methodology, or technique risks disappointment and eventually failure.

Having said that, it should be obvious by now that social labs are not silver-bullet solutions. No course of action or strategy will guarantee a team wins the World Cup. No course of action or strategy will guarantee that we'll be able to address a complex social challenge. All we can do is increase the probabilities of success and avoid courses of action that lead to the mathematical certainty of failure.

The newness of social labs means there is vast scope, not simply for improving things but for true breakthroughs. There is no venerated canon that we are obliged to follow. We don't have to spend years working up to a PhD. We can just get cracking. The vitality of prototyping-based approaches rests in their disregard as to how things *should* be done in favor of what actually works. But as the saying goes, if you're going to break the rules, then break them well and break them beautifully.

Here then are seven rules of thumb for starting social labs. Each can be done in a myriad of ways, and there is no one right way (even as there are plenty of wrong ways). Because these are rules of thumb—not laws—each needs to be shaped by the context of the particular challenge being considered. All successful social labs go through these steps, either consciously or unconsciously.

#1: CLARIFY INTENTION

Dave Fishwick is a successful small-business owner from Burnley in the UK. In 2011 he decided that the banking system was corrupt and needed to change. Banks were not supporting small businesses. So he decided to set up a bank that would lend money to small, local businesses and give all its profits to charity. His method for loaning money was old-fashioned. Instead of a credit check, he would go to speak to business owners.

The government (the Financial Services Authority) didn't want to give Dave a banking license, despite the fact that he personally guaranteed all deposits. A documentary film, called *The Bank of Dave*, showed how he finally got a banking license through running a campaign and is now successfully running the bank, Burnley Savings and Loans Limited. At the end of the documentary, Dave looks into the distance and mumbles, almost as if speaking to himself, "You must never, ever, ever give up."

How badly do you or we want to address a challenge? All practical questions follow from clarity of intention. The high-octane jet fuel required for addressing complex social challenges is intention. There are, of course, lesser fuels—for example, feeling guilty—but these lesser fuels burn out and do not last.

One of my early mentors, Toke Moeller, once remarked, "Clarity of purpose is a sweet weapon against confusion." So how do we clarify intention? Well, there is a range of options to suit the person trying to do so. Conventional approaches involve carving out time to think—ideally taking a sabbatical—and require coming up with ideas and then talking about them with a range of people. Unconventional approaches (or less conventional in terms of the dominant culture) might involve a vision quest or a solo retreat of some sort, away from the hustle and bustle of life. But in either case, clarifying intention requires taking the time to be honest with yourself about what it is that you care about.

The person I learned the most from about clarity of intention was Joseph Jaworski, who has written extensively about his experiences. He once explained to me that intention is like a matchstick—when it flares into light, all the other matchsticks around it also flare, and this chain reaction of intention creates a force that has the capacity to change anything. Intention thus acts as a "strange attractor," and all sorts of help flows toward it.

The education reformist Ken Robinson makes the point, "For most of us the problem isn't that we aim too high and fail—it's just the opposite—we aim too low and succeed."[2]

#2: BROADCAST AN INVITATION

One of the hallmarks of planning culture is sloganeering. The slogan invites people to rise above their petty concerns and to join in. It promises them greatness.

Here's a typical example of a Soviet-era slogan: "Workers of industry! Struggle for the further development and strengthening of the industrial power of our Motherland! Widen the road of new techniques and progressive technologies!"

Here's the twenty-first century equivalent from a European Union–funded initiative (I've changed the name): "Systemic change will not be achieved without the engagement of active citizens. SOCLEVER is a tool for supporting, strengthening, and promoting this engagement and action for systemic change!" (Exclamation mark in original.)

The purpose of the invitation, like the slogan, is to rally people. But there is a key difference. A slogan is propaganda, but an invitation is not. Propaganda aims to "bring about the active or passive participation in its actions of a mass of individuals, psychologically unified through psychological manipulations and incorporated in an organization."[3] Propaganda as a technique for mobilization is unsustainable—because the reasons for participating are shallow and coarse. In other words, when crafting an invitation, don't bullshit. This is even more important if you're good at it.

The invitation is a way of communicating intention. An invitation, in contrast to propaganda, if genuine, is dramatically more effective. We, either as individuals, as leaders, or as organizations, might feel alone in our intention to address a challenge. The question isn't simply how do we convince people to join us, but rather how do we find people who share our intention? The invitation is a way to find people.

Invitations should make clear what the invitation is for. In other words, there is a spectrum between open and closed invitations. An invitation is open if none of the variables have been nailed down and few, if any, decisions have been made. An invitation is closed if all key strategic decisions have been made. The most common mistake is to start completely open. The risk here is that people turn up in response to an invitation only to be asked, "And what would *you* like to do?" Then they look at each other and say, "Uh, we don't know—it's *your* thing." And so on till there's no energy left. In general, it's better to try for somewhere in between, make some key decisions but hold them lightly. "So here's my best guess on these decisions, but do you have a better idea? Is this how we should proceed? Does this make sense?"

If you want to see examples of world-class invitations, look at Kickstarter videos—look at the good ones and the bad ones. These videos are pitches, but they are also invitations to join something. A good invitation is mythic, a call to adventure; it incites romance and excitement, and it raises our game. A good invitation takes craft to get right.

#3: WORK YOUR NETWORKS

As a teenager I used to read the detective series, Alfred Hitchcock and The Three Investigators, which had titles like *The Mystery of the Talking Skull*. The three investigators were kids from Hollywood who would poke into mysteries and solve them. Jupiter, the star investigator, is a bit unfit and likes to read a lot.

A technique Jupiter invents to help in their investigations is called "the ghost-to-ghost hook-up." The idea is very simple. When they want to find out anything, they each call ten friends and ask them. They also ask each of those friends to call ten other friends and ask them the same question. Pretty soon they've mobilized a massive network of thousands of kids to help them. Eventually someone calls back with the answer. ("The man you're looking for lives in Malibu.") A pre-Google Google search.

Once a clear and compelling invitation has been formulated, get it out. Increasingly, the most effective way of getting your invitation out is through your networks, through people who know and trust you, and through your friends. This is the ghost-to-ghost hook-up. Work your networks.

This does not mean sending one mass email and then sitting back. Invite people you know and ask for a conversation, ideally in person. Once they are on board, ask them to invite ten others. Talk to people on the phone, on Skype, and in person. Explain to them what you're doing, why you're doing it, and what you're looking for (people, money, work space, companies, etc.). If they can't help, ask them for names—who do they know who may be interested. If your invitation is good, you'll start seeing results quickly. If your invitation is bad and people are not responding, ask for feedback. Iterate. Remember that getting a result requires a clear ask.

As our public spaces get more and more saturated with advertising, increasingly people will turn to people they know and trust, to their friends and family. Instead of trying to filter the deluge of information we are saturated in ourselves, we will rely on our networks to do it for us.

#4: RECRUIT WILLING PEOPLE

Picture soccer players on the field in flow. They react and respond to attacks; they fall back to defend when needed; they morph and change fluidly depending on what is needed from them. Here's one description of Brazilian soccer:

> In the end you can't capture the power of Brazilian talent in numbers and names. It has to be felt. Every day soccer fans around the world witness the quintessential scene: a group of enemy players surround a Brazilian, leaving him no options, no space, no hope. Then there's a dancelike blur of motion—a feint, a flick, a burst of speed—and suddenly the Brazilian player is in the clear, moving away from his now-tangled opponents with the casual aplomb of a person stepping off a crowded bus.[4]

Imagine now a team that has been built to react and respond to complexity. What would it look like? Just as a football team responds to the challenges faced on the field, a world-class team built for complexity is able to morph, change, and come up with responses where there seem to be "no options, no space, no hope." This then is a vision. How to make it happen, though?

The convening strategy we usually adopt is first to try to find a small group of like-minded organizations or individuals with some convening power. We locate two or three key partners who are willing to lend their names and open their networks up to finding other aligned people. With these key partners, we try to locate at least thirty more individuals, representing different parts of the system we want to impact. From these stakeholders we form a lab team and a secretariat. The number of lab team members typically doesn't exceed thirty-six because it's hard to build trust in a starting group bigger than this.

One of the key challenges with starting to address any complex social challenge is that people will assess the seriousness of an effort. Why should they invest their time and energy in this as opposed to something else? This means that we can spend a lot of our time and energy trying to convince people who are skeptical.

Increasingly, as the nature of power shifts—and so the nature of influence shifts—I'm convinced that we need to spend less time trying to convert people. Instead, we should move on. Obviously there may be actors who are key to the success of our effort, or we *believe* this is so. It isn't necessarily true. Are we going home if a key politician doesn't support us? Really?

Operate on the assumption that the perfect team is out there. We have to go and find them—they won't come and find us. Instead of being blocked by a skeptic, listen carefully and then move on. Go to the next person. If one politician says no, well, there's always another politician to go to. Keep going until you find the right people, and then recruit them. Your problem will more likely be figuring out what to do with all the help you're offered.

The author Seth Godin, who has turned everything we know about marketing on its head, makes this case: "Yes, I think it's okay to abandon the big, established, stuck tribe. It's okay to say to them, 'You're not going where I need to go, and there's no way I'm going to persuade all of you to follow me. So rather than standing here watching the opportunities fade away, I'm heading off. I'm betting some of you, the best of you, will follow me.'"[5]

#5: SET DIRECTION

In 1998 the LEGO Group owned one of the world's most recognized and successful brands, the Lego brick. Sales, however, were slowing as kids turned to online games and other forms of virtual play. Turnaround expert Poul Plougmann, formerly of Bang & Olufsen, was brought in as CEO to revive the flagging fortunes of this immensely successful group. He took to his task by launching an ambitious innovation-centric initiative. Plough-mann attempted to implement "the seven truths of innovation," which included "hire diverse and creative people" and "practice disruptive innovation." The results were catastrophic. By the end of 2003 the company was losing cash so fast there was real doubt it would survive 2004.

Plougmann was fired. His replacements were given the task of saving the firm. These were two unlikely characters—the new CEO, Jorgen Vig Knudstorp, and CFO Jesper Ovesen. Both were relative newcomers to a group composed of people who had been there decades. Knudstorp was a former McKinsey consultant who had become a roving strategist within the group. Ovesen was a seasoned CFO, formerly of a respected Danish bank. Both had played instrumental roles in diagnosing for the board the dire reality of LEGO Group's situation.

Professor David Robertson, who studied the LEGO story, recounts a dinner meeting they had:

> "I had something like eight proposals on what to do about operations, seven proposals for market actions and so forth," exclaimed Knudstorp. "In all, I must have proposed fifty or sixty actions. And Jesper just looked at me and said, 'The way you describe the company and the way I understand the situation, your plan is too complex. It's never going to happen.'" Ovesen's advice was direct as it was taut: Forget strategy. The company needed an action plan for survival.[6]

Instead of coming up with a grand strategic vision or plan, Knudstorp and Ovesen set a strategic direction—survival—and then went about doing what was needed for the group to survive. This is not a new idea in business. Gary Hamel and CK Prahalad wrote about the importance of "strategic intent" almost two decades ago in the pages of *Harvard Business Review*.[7]

Complex social challenges are too complicated for grand strategies. Instead, what is required from conveners of social labs is strategic direction and the creation of space. Within that space unfold multiple actions aligned in a strategic direction. That's strategy.

#6: DESIGN IN STACKS

All the social labs involve multiple activities. In the labs I've worked on, these activities were divided into different layers, or stacks.

1. *Innovation or problem solving:* In the labs we have run, the basis for this layer has been the U Process.

2. *Information and learning:* This involves research, baseline surveys, documenting the process of the lab, and disseminating results.

3. *Capacity building:* This could involve building the capacity of the lab team or the secretariat.

4. *Governance:* This may consist of a formal legal structure, or it may involve a steering committee or leadership group of some sort. Warning: overdo this one at your peril.

Design your lab in stacks, and design a stack only when you need one. In other words, don't spend years planning your perfect lab on paper. Sketch out roughly what each stack might look like and its parameters. Then flesh them out and build them as and when needed.

There are endless options in terms of how, where, and when to design your stacks. For example, you may decide to run multiple innovation or problem-solving stacks, maybe in different neighborhoods, or with different demographics. Or you may decide to invite a partner to help design and run the information stack.

#7: FIND CADENCE

The issues are so heartbreaking and situations so urgent that the space of addressing complex social challenges is rife with burnout. One of the most difficult lessons I've learned in running social labs is about timing, and in particular, cadence.

Cadence is a term used in agile project management to refer to a pace that's sustainable. An agile coach, Mike Cottmeyer, coined the mantra, "Stable Velocity. Sustainable Pace." The origins of the term *cadence* come from the world of cycling. When professional cyclists are tackling particularly difficult stretches, they search for cadence, a rhythm of pedaling that is sustainable. Consider the case of the novice cyclist who changes gears while going uphill and gets pitched over the handlebars. That's anti-cadence, if you like.

When we first started using agile approaches, it seemed like an impossible struggle. Initially, we just flailed about like a first-time cyclist hitting a steep, steep hill. People on the team questioned the process, asking if it made sense and why we were doing it. Persistence and learning are rewarded by the magic of cadence— hitting a rhythm of activity that's stable, and hence sustainable. Finding cadence is not easy, but teams that find it can climb up any hill.

Recently, while convening a lab, one of our advisors said that the trick was to "make haste slowly."[8] And that's the key. Push, but don't be aggressive. Keep going, find cadence, and you're on your way.

CONCLUSION
Next-Generation Social Labs

A zombie idea is one that keeps coming back, despite being killed.

— John Quiggin

Indeed, one concern would be that the initial neoconservative response to a zombie outbreak would be to invade Iraq again out of force of habit.

— Daniel W. Drezner

In puzzling over the situation in Yemen, I started seeing planning as a zombie idea. The planning paradigm, despite being killed many times over, for example, with the death of the Soviet Union, still walks among us. And it keeps biting the living, turning them into the undead.

Planning is ubiquitous across sectors, operating horizontally in the state and vertically down corporate and civil society supply and service chains. Planning was—and remains—a means of centralized control of resources, labor, and outputs by a small number of technocrats. It's the favored means of responding to complexity. Yet it's badly suited to the challenges we now face.

As a result of repeatedly applying the planning paradigm, we are in the midst of a worldwide crisis, a crisis of capital—human, social, natural, and financial. This crisis has the potential to take us all the way to widespread societal collapse. And the reason for this collapse is a zombie idea—planning.

Welcome to the zombie apocalypse.

AVERTING THE ZOMBIE APOCALYPSE

In Yemen we have an archetypical situation characterized by complexity that unfortunately represents a plausible future for many of us. What does it mean to blow the carrying capacity of a country? What does it look like to be running out of resources, such as water and energy, while the population grows exponentially? What happens when a security situation leads to a drone war? It looks a lot like Yemen. And it doesn't look good. It looks like a country heading in slow motion for a full-blown zombie apocalypse. Elements of what we're seeing in Yemen are happening all over the place, mirrored on a planetary scale.

Hawaii's Mauna Loa observatory recently reported that measurements of atmospheric CO_2 had breached the barrier of 400 parts per million.[1] The implications of this are being hotly debated. They include permanent food shortages resulting in 40-percent price hikes, the melting of the Siberian tundra leading to massive releases of methane, and a billion climate refugees. Meanwhile the world's governments are locked into paralysis, unable to agree on a plan. Even if they settle on one, there is very little hope of successfully implementing it. The situation looks, in short, a lot like a global zombie apocalypse.

So how could social labs help avert this apocalypse? There are three strategic responses based on the ideas presented in this book—*stabilization, mitigation,* and *adaptation.* Again, these are not silver bullets, but they demonstrate that practical responses are well within our means.

STATE COLLAPSE: A STABILIZATION STRATEGY

The situation in Yemen has simultaneously improved and deteriorated. Incumbent President Saleh agreed to resign as part of an internationally brokered deal, seen to be averting a potential civil war. A new president, Hadi Mansour, has been sworn in, pledging reform and convening a national dialogue leading to a new constitution. A month after he took over, the worst suicide bombing in Sanaa killed 120 soldiers and injured hundreds more. The overall security situation, coupled with the inexorable resource crisis, continues to slide.

During all this, a strategy evolved from our many conversations with both Yemenis and non-Yemenis. The idea, representing a possible strategic direction, is *state stabilization* through *sectoral stabilization*. The idea of sectoral stabilization is to identify sectors critical to Yemen's survival—food, agriculture, water, health care, energy, and so on—and focus efforts on them. If these sectors can be stabilized, this ensures against state failure, regardless of what happens at the level of the regime.

How could this work? Multi-stakeholder teams of Yemenis are convened around each sector, drawing in actors from government, the business community, and civil society. These stakeholder teams (the equivalent of lab teams) are then tasked with stabilizing their particular sector. Each carefully selected team is given a degree of autonomous decision making in order to decide what actions need to be undertaken in order to stabilize their sector. They are provided with cash, as well as negotiation and technical support. They are invited to implement on a monthly cycle, to be renewed annually. The fund is provided by the Saudis or the Gulf States and allows Yemenis to self-determine how it is to be spent via a process such as described above.

The strategy is social, in that it shifts the locus of efforts purely from already-stretched government technocrats to a wider stakeholder base—almost an extended team supporting the government to achieve their goals. The process we are proposing is experimental, in that stakeholder groups get an opportunity to figure out and test what works on the ground. And finally, the approach is systemic, in that it attempts to address the causal challenges of key sectors in Yemen.

One of the challenges in working on the issue has been including Yemenis in the initiative early on. This could be interpreted as picking a side, and we would risk losing our neutrality as facilitators. Our approach so far has been outside in, starting by lobbying external stakeholders and approaching the Yemenis only when we felt we had something to offer.

A partnership emerged during the course of our work. Oxfam introduced us to Integrity Research and Consulting, run by Anthony Ellis, a former foreign office official who served in places like Afghanistan and, briefly, Yemen. Integrity specializes in conducting research in conflict zones, where they aim for 90 percent of the work to be done by local researchers (as opposed to expats).

Anthony, in turn, introduced us to Omnia Strategy, Cherie Blair's firm. At our first meeting, Blair walked in the room and demanded, "What's this about? We need another report on Yemen like a hole in the head." This was followed by an hour of expertly poised questions and answers. At the end of the meeting, she and her business partner, Sofia Wellesley, approved of the action-oriented approach we were proposing and provided much-needed support.

Together we met with the Yemeni ambassador in London and

formally presented our strategy to the Yemeni government. The next step is to brief the relevant ministers and then eventually the president. The implications of such a direction for other nation-states, such as many Arab Spring countries, is vast and provides a strategy for stabilization in many countries suffering from a strategic vacuum.

CLIMATE CHANGE: A MITIGATION STRATEGY

The fact that in 2013 atmospheric CO_2 breached 400 parts per million carries profound implications. Even if emissions were to stop cold today, we would still be looking at a future where the polar caps melt and sea levels rise. In the United States alone, some 1400 cities are under threat.[2] Such reports on the dangers of climate change proliferate, painting a world of permanent food shortages and temperatures in Australia as high as 50°C (122°F), which would lead to the largest spontaneous bushfires ever seen.[3] Economist Lord Nicholas Stern admitted, "I got it wrong on climate change—it's far, far worse."[4]

According to scientific estimates, global emissions need to peak very soon, between 2015 and 2020. However, with emissions steadily increasing every year, we are squarely on a BAU trajectory leading to a truly frightening situation—temperature increases of 4–6°C (or about 41°F). This will result in widespread ecosystem collapse. There are few, if any, grounded strategies in play around peaking.

As part of my work with the Climate Action Network, a potential peaking strategy emerged from hundreds of conversations. We call it the Gigatonne Lab, or the GT Lab. The idea is to bring together a group of policy makers, financial experts, and technologists to attempt to reduce global equivalent carbon dioxide (CO_2e) emissions by one gigatonne (GT) within a two-year time frame. Current global emissions are close to 49 GT CO_2e per year. One GT represents approximately the entire annual emissions footprint for Germany or the continent of Africa.

We soft-tested the idea for almost two years, ironing out details and iterating it to take into account feedback. Convening the lab began in July 2013. We drew up a list of about a hundred people and sent them a short outline of the lab—the invitation. We asked them if they were interested or if they knew anyone who might be interested in the lab, either as a co-convener, a lab team member, an advisor, or a funder.

Within a few short weeks, we got a tremendous response back. We spoke to a range of actors, all of whom thought the idea was intriguing, if fraught with practical challenges. Time and time again, we were interrogated with sharp questions about how the lab would work. We presented our best guess and invited actors to help nail down some of the more difficult strategic decisions that needed to be made.

We started sketching out the lab's possible stacks. We imagined several regional innovation layers, each responsible for a significant chunk of emissions. For example, a California Gigatonne Lab and a Canada Gigatonne Lab could each be responsible for figuring out how to achieve a part of the gigatonne target.

We spoke to campaigning organizations about running a public campaign around the gigatonne target, with the idea of inviting the general public into a wider conversation about how to reduce emissions by a gigatonne in two years. The lab acts as a public platform, a sprint to achieve emissions reduction in practice, thereby demonstrating that it's possible to rapidly decarbonize. If the lab works, it could spawn layers, each contributing against a set baseline to significantly reduce global emissions.

One vision is to have several dozen multiple autonomous or

semi-autonomous GT Labs around the world, each making significant contributions to emissions reduction, a solution that could be thought of as "fast, cheap and out of control."[5] The GT Lab could point the way to a global peaking strategy.

COMMUNITY RESILIENCE: AN ADAPTATION STRATEGY

Communities around the world are subject to increasing shocks. These shocks range from the environmental, such as extreme weather events, to the fiscal, where public services are cut. In some cases these shocks are predictable. In the UK, for example, it's possible to figure out which communities will be hardest hit by cuts to public services, such as health care, well in advance of the cuts occurring. Where climate change is concerned, we are starting to see patterns—repeated flooding and heat waves causing extreme damage to property and, in the worse cases, loss of life.

Early in 2012 we were approached by Alan Heeks—a social entrepreneur, writer, and consultant with a passion for sustainability in the fullest sense. Alan was concerned about how communities across the UK would cope with a number of shocks, including social, environmental, and economic. He wanted to know if we could help come up with a response that would practically increase the resilience of communities to these shocks. In our first conversation, I asked Alan, "Which communities?" He looked at me, surprised, and said, "All of them."

It took a year of work to figure out an approach. We did extensive research, which included interviews with thinkers and actors within the broad field of resilience, examining a range of existing initiatives (we created an "atlas of resilience strategies" to map them), and a number of consultations. The Community Resilience Lab was born out of this approach.

The core idea behind the lab is to bring together stakeholders around particular geographies in order to come up with proactive responses to the resilience challenges they face. Instead of waiting for a shock to hit the community and then mobilizing a post-event response, the goal is to tackle challenges before they hit.

THE BATTLE OF THE PARTS VERSUS THE WHOLE

In an essay critiquing optimization in the Soviet Union, Cosma Shalizi writes,

> These are all going to be complex problems, full of messy compromises. Attaining even second best solutions is going to demand "bold, persistent experimentation," coupled with a frank recognition that many experiments will just fail, and that even long-settled compromises can, with the passage of time, become confining obstacles. We will not be able to turn everything over to the wise academicians, or even to their computers, but we may, if we are lucky and smart, be able, bit by bit, to make a world fit for human beings to live in.[6]

A social lab is a gathering, a coming together of people across the silos that characterize dominant social structures in order to attend to a social challenge for as long as necessary to shift the situation. In the face of the technocratic systems of high modernism, the paradigm of the social lab lives and dies by an idea that perhaps seem quaint in this day and age—the idea that people working together can address our most profound challenges.

A critical underlying condition behind the success of a social lab is that as much as possible, the people on the lab team act of their own volition, a lot like world class athletes. It's clear that as adults, we will not really change the way they see, listen, talk, embody, and collaborate unless they are self-directed enough to know why they are doing these things. They are, in effect, committed to shifting a system and creating social change not because they were forced to by a central authority or because they are being paid to but because they believe in the need to shift a system from its current state to a desired state.

Social labs therefore require that participants operate from a place of inner volition and drive. In doing so, we are creating a space for people to connect to their deeper calling for change, for a better state of affairs. This inner volition, independent of institutional authority, is ultimately what makes the change that comes from a social lab sustainable.

By definition, a social lab must be *social*. That is, participants of the lab are not simply experts, whether they're academics or activists. Rather, team members must reflect the diversity of the stakeholders concerned with the issue at hand.

In order to justify being a *lab*, a social lab must also undertake to work in an experimental and iterative way to address challenges. A program is very different from a lab.

Finally, for social labs to actually have impact, they must be systemic in orientation, aiming to address social issues at their root cause. Labs, whatever their focus, must put inquiry—and not just advocacy—at the heart of their activities.

Our most ferocious challenge today is to avoid the reactionary tendency to go to war with our problems. As Max Dublin reminds us, "All failures in achieving goals, that is, in mastery, be they in our ability to build cars or to make love, are based on failures in cultivation, in nurturance." We have a tendency to declare hugely catastrophic wars against our social challenges. The war on drugs is just one example.

The attractions of war, however, are that it's glorious, it's heroic, and it's human. War brings out something both terrible and human within us, and we are drawn to it as a way out of having to focus on ourselves, on our failures in cultivation and nurturance. The call to arms in the name of justice is most dangerous and seductive. From the Crusades to the war in Iraq, wars have been fought under the banner of a higher calling.

As our social challenges become more serious, we will find ourselves subject to new siren songs calling us to fight new crusades.

Social labs represent the constitution of a new sphere of activity, a new space. The gathering together of people within this space represents the beginning of what can be thought of as an armistice, a suspension of what has been called *the battle of the parts versus the whole*. People come together, recognizing the truth that the cost of war is too high and there is another way.

ACKNOWLEDGMENTS

There is a great joy that comes from working on things that, well, work. The last fifteen years of this purposeful effort has been extraordinarily hard in so many ways. Spending so much time head down in the weeds makes it very difficult to know if progress is being made. It's hard to know if our multiple investments in time, money, sweat, and tears are going to pay off; if we're moving in the right direction; or if we're about to fall screaming off a cliff. But I learned that innovation is not simply a flash of insight but hard work. And there's a reason why the work is hard. Through the doubt and confusion, a magical coherence emerges. The constant vigilance that is required can be exhausting for everyone involved. That vigilance, however, offers unparalleled rewards. These rewards are akin to cresting a hill, footsore, exhausted, and with an aching heart, only to be confronted with a stunning vista, a view of the sun spearing the vast and endless sea. I have been extraordinarily blessed to share such moments time and time again with many people.

A first book based on a decade of practice tends to accrue a few debts. There are so many of you to thank.

First, I'd like to thank Mia Eisenstadt, my wife, partner, and first reader. This book is just one product of our partnership. It wouldn't have happened intellectually, energetically, or practically without your generous spirit. Thank you.

I'd like to thank my dad for my earliest lessons in persistence and integrity and for encouraging me to stop reading Robert Ludlum and start reading the Russian classics. You remain my hero. I'd like to thank my mum, who taught me how to write and who has supported me unconditionally on this winding road. I'd like to thank my siblings: my twin sister, Shagufta, for standing over me and defending me from the time we were toddlers; my younger sister, Shafaq, for her love and for inspiring me with her strength; and my younger brother, Faraz, for his unwavering support and for the clarity of his faith. Thank you, Rasheed, my brother-in-law, for both emotional and intellectual support.

I'd like to thank the tribe of my in-laws, the Eisenstadts, for their constant and cheerful support. Thanks to Marc, who read endless drafts of this book and helped make it stronger. Thanks to Jacqueline for her energy, enthusiasm, and practical support— it really wouldn't have happened without you. Thanks to Leo for all his hard work—man, you know better than anyone else the insanity of this trip. Thanks to Nathan for all the late-night philosophical conversations and references. Thanks to Charlotte for your thoughtfulness and warmth. Thanks to Naomi for taking the time to read multiple, extremely long, early drafts and for patiently talking me through it all. Thanks to Eric for your detailed feedback and support.

I'd like to thank all my colleagues, past and present, at Reos Partners. It's been a singular inspiration to work with all of you. Thanks to Menka Sangvi for all your care, ongoing support, and feedback on the book. Thanks to Charlie O'Malley for your energy, hard work, and feedback. Thanks, Mia and Leo, for your multiple roles. Thank you all for being my colleagues.

Thanks to Yve Field for your "big question" and for being an inspiration. Many thanks to Mike Kang for all the feedback on the book and for being a rock. Thanks to Jonathan Ekin for all your work on the Gigatonne Lab—you're a model of persistence that we should all be following. Thanks to Sean Legassick for our decade of friendship, for your presence, and for all your feedback on the book. Thanks Hendrik, for holding the labs flag through thick and thin. Thanks to Henry Thompson for being an extraordinary teacher. Thanks to Jeff Stottlemyer for your friendship and good cheer. Thanks to Nathan Heintz for the Tao. Thanks, Alexandra Yannias and Rachel Caines, for all the research over the years—it's been gold. Thanks to our associates, in particular Cat Tulley, Dharmesh Mistry, Schirin Yachkaschi, as well as Caroline Rennie (for the feedback) and Martin Down.

I'd like to thank Adam Kahane for taking a punt on me all those years ago, for showing me the ropes, for your unfailing support, and most of all, for your patience, which sometimes feels deep as the earth. Thank you for playing the unforgiving role of being an intellectual foil. I'd like to thank Mille Bojer for being a mirror over the last fifteen years and, above all, for being my friend through it all. I'd like to thank Joe McCarron for warmth, for our many great conversations over the years, and for helping me think through the practicalities of social labs—there's a lot of your head, heart, and hands in this book.

Thanks to Colleen Magner—for your feedback on the book, your friendship, and for encouraging me to write all those years ago at Borl. Thanks to LeAnne Grillo—you're a bright shining star. Thanks to my Dutch colleagues, Batian, Lenneke, Mariette, and Jos, for being exemplary colleagues and for your helpful feedback. Thanks to my Australian colleagues, Steve and Leigh, for the feedback and Southern cheer. Thanks to Christel, Vanessa, and Rebecca for your clear feedback. Thanks to Maianne Knuth, for love and integrity but, in particular, for the call that put me on this path. Thanks to Jeff Barnum for being my long-suffering friend and for being infuriatingly right most of the time. Thanks to Lorna for all your hard work on comms. Thanks to Matt Gelbwaks, for your friendship and for introducing me to a whole new world.

Thanks to my brother-in-arms, Mustafa Suleyman, for your love and for your fire.

Thanks to all my former colleagues at Generon. Thanks to Joseph Jaworksi at Generon International—I continue to learn from you and miss you. Thanks to Susan Taylor for a decade of love and support. Thanks to Grady McGonagill for your feedback on the book and long-standing support. Thanks to the late Tom Rautenberg, who passed in 2012. I met Tom early on this journey. I carry him with me.

Thanks to Otto Scharmer for your intellectual generosity. I've been profoundly shaped by it.

Thanks, Joi Ito at the MIT Media Lab, for the foreword. Big thanks to Ethan Zuckerman for your largesse of spirit and for putting shoulder to the wheel. Thanks to Jessica for facilitating it all.

Thanks to all of our partners. Thanks to Anthony Ellis and Kate Ives from Integrity. Thanks for all the generosity, Cherie Blair and Sofia Wellesley at Omnia.

Thanks, Anna Lau, for the research support and keeping me connected to the scene. Thanks, Ann Yoachim, for the friendship, for your insights, and for helping me think through it all. Thanks to Habiba Hamed for your energy and my crash course on UAE politics. Thanks to Louise Scovell for setting the aesthetic bar and for all your unwavering support. Thanks to Cari Caldwell and AJ Pape for your support and good humor. Thanks to Maikel Lieuw Kie Song for all the conversations and the friendship.

Thanks to all of our clients. Without you, none of this would have been possible.

Thanks to everyone else who read an early draft of the book and gave me invaluable feedback, in alphabetical order: Alhassan Adam, Fode Beaudet, David Bent, Chris Cavanagh, Rabea Chaudhary Amin, Benjamin Degenhart, Lilly Evans, Peter Feltham, Bob Stilger, Kelly Teamey, Henry Thompson, Shannon Walbran, and Angela Wilkinson.

Thanks to the one hundred plus people who gave feedback and input on the title and the cover. There are too many of you to thank individually here, but I remain immensely grateful.

Finally, humble thanks to Steve Piersanti from Berrett-Koehler. Steve, this book would rightfully not have seen the light of day without your generous wisdom. Thank you. To all my new-found colleagues at Berrett-Koehler: Jeevan, Kristen, Marina, Michael, Zoe, Maria, Steve, Dave, and others a big thanks for all you're doing and about to do. A special thanks to Dianne for all the hard work on the cover. Thanks to my BK reviewers, Nic Albert, Charlotte Ashlock, Sam Garner, Anna Leinberger, and Carrie Rich—your feedback was invaluable. Last, big thanks to Tanya Grove for all her patient copy-editing and to David Peattie for stewarding this book along its final stages with so much patience. Finally, thanks to all the people who took the trouble to write such generous endorsements. Thank you.

NOTES

Preface

1. https://en.wikipedia.org/wiki/Grounded_theory.

Introduction

1. Zygmunt Bauman, *Liquid Modernity* (Polity, 2000).
2. Thomas Homer-Dixon, "Complexity Science and Public Policy," www.homerdixon.com/2010/05/05/complexity=science=and=public =policy/
3. Nina Munk, *The Idealist: Jeffrey Sachs and the Quest to End Poverty* (Doubleday, 2013).
4. Peter M. Senge, *The Fifth Discipline: The Art & Practice of the Learning Organization*, Revised & Updated ed. (Doubleday, 2006).
5. Susan Sweitzer, "Learning History—Chapter 4" (Paper presented at the Sustainable Food Laboratory, 2005).
6. Simon Zadek, *The Civil Corporation: The New Economy of Corporate Citizenship* (Earthscan Ltd, 2001).
7. Hal Hamilton, Eric Lowitt, and Jan Kees Vis, "Chapter Four: Renewing the Global Food System," in *The Collaboration Economy: How to Meet Business, Social, and Environmental Needs and Gain Competitive Advantage* (Jossey-Bass, 2013).
8. Steven Levy, *In the Plex: How Google Thinks, Works, and Shapes Our Lives* (Simon & Schuster, 2011).
9. Michael Lewis, *Moneyball* (W.W. Norton & Company, 2011).
10. http://www.powershow.com/view/3b8d8a-NTYoM/Dreyfus_

Model_of_Skill_Acquisition_Craig_McClure_MD_EOS_
powerpoint_ppt_presentation.

11. Marianne Knuth, "Kago Ya Bana: Three Years of Working for Children in Midvaal" (Paper presented at the Kago Ya Bana, 2010).

12. Albert-László Bonabeau and Eric Barabási, "Scale-Free Networks," *Scientific American* (2003).

13. Abhijit Banerjee and Esther Duflo, *Poor Economics: A Radical Rethinking of the Way to Fight Global Poverty*, Reprint (PublicAffairs, 2012).

14. http://www.resilientjapan.org/.

15. http://www.rmi.org/elab.

16. http://www.open-contracting.org/.

17. http://fab.cba.mit.edu/.

Chapter 1

1. http://data.worldbank.org/country/yemen-republic.

2. For more on Yemen, see Victoria Clark, *Yemen: Dancing on the Heads of Snakes* (Yale University Press, 2010); Gregory D. Johnsen, *The Last Refuge: Yemen, Al-Qaeda, and the Battle for Arabia* (Oneworld Publications, 2013); and Isa Blumi, *Chaos in Yemen: Societal Collapse and the New Authoritarianism*, Reprint (Routledge, 2012).

3. Melanie Mitchell, *Complexity: A Guided Tour* (Oxford University Press, USA, 2009).

4. For an outline of the information challenge we face, see Nate Silver, *The Signal and the Noise: The Art and Science of Prediction* (Allen Lane, 2012).

5. Nate Silver, *The Signal and the Noise: Why So Many Predictions Fail — But Some Don't* (Penguin Press HC, 2012).

6. Ronald A. Heifetz et al., *The Practice of Adaptive Leadership: Tools and Tactics for Changing Your Organization and the World* (Harvard Business Press, 2009).

7. Horst W. J. Rittel and Melvin M. Webber, "Dilemmas in a General Theory of Planning," *Policy Sciences* 4 (1973): 155–69.

8. David Schmaltz, *The Blind Men and the Elephant: Mastering Project Work* (Berrett-Koehler Publishers, 2003).

9. Rod Hill & Tony Myatt, *The Economics Anti-Textbook: A Critical Thinker's Guide to Microeconomics* (Zed Books, 2010).

10. See Francis Spufford, *Red Plenty* (Faber and Faber, 2011) for an account of the Soviet Union and a utopia built on the idea of optimization.

11. Ramez Naam, *The Infinite Resource: The Power of Ideas on a Finite Planet* (UPNE, 2013).

12. I first heard this phrase from Alex Steffan, "Winning the Great Wager," http://www.worldchanging.com/archives/002197.html.

13. "The Yemeni elite is comprised of tribal sheiks, military leaders, religious leaders, political party elites, technocrats and, to a lesser degree, traditional merchants. These elites are responsible for setting and pursuing the national agenda, though this is not necessarily to imply that the interests of the elite are aligned with the interests of the average citizen. Broadly speaking, Yemen's political elites are not developmentally inclined, particularly as one moves up the regime's hierarchy, although there are some exceptions to this." Sarah Phillips, *Yemen and the Politics of Permanent Crisis* (Adelphi Series) (Routledge, 2011).

14. Janine R. Wedel, *Shadow Elite: How the World's New Power Brokers Undermine Democracy, Government, and the Free Market* (Basic Books, 2009).

15. Juan Pablo Cardenal and Heriberto Araujo, *China's Silent Army: The Pioneers, Traders, Fixers and Workers Who Are Remaking the World in Beijing's Image* (Crown, 2013).

16. Robert Worth, "Is Yemen the Next Afghanistan?" *NY Times Magazine* (2010).

17. Jared Diamond and James A. Robinson, *Natural Experiments of History*, Reprint (Harvard University Press, 2011).

18. Chatham House, "Development Assistance and Humanitarian Aid," *Yemen: Political Dynamics and the International Policy Framework*, http://www.youtube.com/watch?v=DUHeJYJwd-A.

19. Andrew Ross Sorkin, *Too Big to Fail: The Inside Story of How Wall Street and Washington Fought to Save the Financial System—and Themselves* (Penguin Books, 2011).

20. "Sir Mervyn King: 'Too Big to Fail, Too Big to Jail or Simply Too Big,'" BBC Business News (June 19, 2013).

Chapter 2

1. Randy Shilts, *And the Band Played On: Politics, People, and the AIDS Epidemic, 20th-Anniversary Edition* (St. Martin's Griffin, 2007).

2. Ibid.

3. Nakoda Mini-Lab, March 3–5, 2004, Proceedings (unpublished project document).

4. "The traditional bilateral/multilateral/NGO triumvirate now repre-

sents a rapidly reducing percentage of national budgets in recipient countries. Bilateral aid budgets have seen significant drops in, for example, the Netherlands, although with increases in Australia and the UK. In all cases, aid budgets are much more intensely scrutinised, given the global financial crisis. Strengthened local economies in Africa, Asia and Latin America—and more fragile economies in Europe and North America—are shifting power relations." "The Politics of Evidence Conference Report" (Paper presented at the The Politics of Evidence Conference, 2013).

5. Gwyn Bevan (Lse), Christopher Hood (Oxford), "What's Measured Is What Matters: Targets and Gaming in the English Public Health Care System," Discussion Paper Series: No. 0501 (2005).

6. See "Six Ways to Die," a model by Vinay Gupta, www.appropedia .org/Six_ways_to_die.

7. Ilan Kapoor, *Celebrity Humanitarianism: The Ideology of Global Charity* (Routledge, 2012).

8. Michael Barnett, *Empire of Humanity: A History of Humanitarianism* (Cornell University Press, 2013).

9. Linda Polman, *War Games: The Story of Aid and War in Modern Times* (Viking, 2011).

10. Thomas G. Weiss, *Humanitarian Business* (Polity Press, 2013).

11. Richard A. Clarke and Robert Knake, *Cyber War: The Next Threat to National Security and What to Do About It* (Ecco, 2011).

12. Patrick F. Gillham, Bob Edwards, and John A. Noakes, "Strategic Incapacitation and the Policing of Occupy Wall Street Protests in New York City, 2011," *Policing and Society: An International Journal of Research and Policy* Vol. 23, Issue 1 (2012).

13. Emile Simpson, *War from the Ground Up: Twenty-First Century Combat as Politics* (C Hurst & Co Publishers Ltd, 2012).

14. Linda J. Bilmes, "The Financial Legacy of Iraq and Afghanistan: How Wartime Spending Decisions Will Constrain Future National Security Budgets," *HKS Faculty Research Working Paper Series RWP13-006* (2013).

15. David H. Price, *Weaponizing Anthropology: Social Science in Service of the Militarized State* (AK Press, 2011); Roberto J. Gonzalez, *American Counterinsurgency: Human Science and the Human Terrain* (Prickly Paradigm Press, 2009).

16. Henry Mintzberg, *The Rise and Fall of Strategic Planning* (Financial Times Prentice Hall, 2000).

17. Ibid.

18. Bent Flyvbjerg, *Rationality and Power: Democracy in Practice* (University of Chicago Press, 1998).

19. Mintzberg, The Rise and Fall of Strategic Planning.

20. Constantine Sandis and Nassim Nicholas Taleb, "Ethics and Asymmetry: Skin in the Game as a Required Heuristic for Acting Under Uncertainty," www.fooledbyrandomness.com/SandisTaleb.pdf.

21. Zaid Hassan, "Slouching Towards Flatlands," *What's the Real Story? Generating a Dialogue around the MDGs* (2008).

22. Ulrich Beck, *Risk Society: Towards a New Modernity* (SAGE Publications Ltd, 1992).

23. Pierre Bourdieu, *The Logic of Practice* (Polity Press, 1992).

24. Bourdieu describes *habitus* as "systems of durable, transposable dispositions, structured structures predisposed to function as structuring structures, that is, as principles which generate and organize practices and representations that can be objectively adapted to their outcomes without presupposing a conscious aiming at ends or an express mastery of the operations necessary to attain them. Objectively 'regulated' and 'regular' without being in any way the product of obedience to rules, they can be collectively orchestrated without being the product of an organizing action of a conductor."

25. Bourdieu, *The Logic of Practice*.

Chapter 3

1. See Heifetz et al., *The Practice of Adaptive Leadership: Tools and Tactics for Changing Your Organization and the World* for a distinction between leadership and authority.

2. This paper was known as the "Red Book," and it was the seminal paper informing our thinking on first-generation social labs. The Leadership Lab outlined here is the model for Change Labs that we followed. C. Otto Scharmer and Joseph Jaworski, "Leadership in the Digital Economy: Sensing and Actualizing Emerging Futures."

3. C. Otto Scharmer, *Theory U: Leading from the Future as It Emerges* (Berrett-Koehler Publishers, 2009).

4. Zaid Hassan, "Connecting to Source," *The Systems Thinker* Vol 17, No 7 (2006).

5. See http://worldwildlife.org/industries/sustainable-agriculture.

6. http://www.un.org/apps/news/story.asp?NewsID=45165#
.UflIbGRoQjE.

7. Deepak Ray et al., "Yield Trends Are Insufficient to Double Global
Crop Production by 2050," *PLOS ONE* 8, no. 6 (2013).

8. Center for Investigative Reporting, 2012, #98911 See http://cironline
.org/reports/hidden-costs-hamburgers-3701.

9. Susan Sweitzer, "Learning History—Chapter 3" (Paper presented at
the Sustainable Food Laboratory, 2005).

10. Donella H. Meadows et al., *The Limits to Growth: The 30-Year Update* (Routledge, 2004).

11. Susan Sweitzer, "Learning History—Chapter 1" (Paper presented at
the Sustainable Food Laboratory, 2004).

12. Sweitzer, "Learning History—Chapter 1."

13. Adam Kahane, *Transformative Scenario Planning: Working Together
to Change the Future* (Berrett-Koehler Publishers, 2012).

14. Doug Reeler, "A Theory of Social Change and Implications for
Practice, Planning, Monitoring and Evaluation" (2007).

Chapter 4

1. Joseph Jaworski, *Source: The Inner Path of Knowledge Creation*
(Berrett-Koehler Publishers, 2012).

2. Tom Rautenberg, "Private Memo to Vision Team, Gang of Five,
and Surita Sandosham" (2006).

3. Professor James C. Scott, *Domination and the Arts of Resistance: Hidden Transcripts* (Yale University Press, 1992).

4. Vrinda Datta and Joyeeta Sengupta, *Evaluation Reports of the
Maharashtra Change Lab Process* (Mumbai: Tata Institute of Social
Sciences, 2006).

5. Adam Kahane, *Power and Love: A Theory and Practice of Social
Change* (Berrett-Koehler Publishers, 2010).

6. Anna Lowenhaupt Tsing, *Friction: An Ethnography of Global Connection* (Princeton University Press, 2004).

Chapter 5

1. Tom sadly passed away on February 19, 2012.

2. http://www.synergos.org/knowledge/12/bhavishyaalliancelegacyand
learning.pdf

3. Anganwadi means "courtyard shelter" in Hindi. They are part of the

Indian Integrated Child Development Services program to combat child hunger and malnutrition.

4. UNICEF, "Significant Improvement in Nutrition Status for Maharashtra's Children Under-Two," http://www.unicef.org/india/Nutrition_Maharashtra.docx.

5. John Michael Greer, "How Civilizations Fall: A Theory of Catabolic Collapse," http://www.ecoshock.org/transcripts/greer_on_collapse.pdf.

6. Ibid.

7. Elinor Ostrom argues: "The concept of social capital should take its place alongside physical and human capital as core concepts of great usefulness to the social sciences." Ostrom defines three broad forms of social capital "important in the study of collective action." These are (1) trustworthiness, (2) networks, and (3) formal and informal rules for institutions. Social labs have generated precisely such forms of social capital, and it's these forms of social capital, according to Ostrom, that "contribute to successful collective action."

8. Steve Denning, "The Dumbest Idea in the World: Maximizing Shareholder Value," http://www.forbes.com/sites/stevedenning/2011/11/28/maximizing-shareholder-value-the-dumbest-idea-in-the-world/.

9. Peter Buffett, "The Charitable-Industrial Complex," *New York Times*, July 26, 2013.

10. Dan Pallotta, "The Way We Think about Charity Is Dead Wrong," http://www.ted.com/talks/dan_pallotta_the_way_we_think_about_charity_is_dead_wrong.html.

11. Buffett, "The Charitable-Industrial Complex."

12. Milford Bateman, *Why Doesn't Microfinance Work? The Destructive Rise of Local Neoliberalism* (Zed Books Ltd., 2010).

13. Lewis Hyde, *Common as Air: Revolution, Art, and Ownership* (Farrar, Straus and Giroux, 2010).

14. Victor W. Hwang, *The Rainforest: The Secret to Building the Next Silicon Valley* (Regenwald, 2012).

15. See Chap 1, James C. Scott, *Seeing Like a State: How Certain Schemes to Improve the Human Condition Have Failed* (Yale University Press, 1999).

Chapter 6

1. Bent Flyvbjerg, *Making Social Science Matter* (Cambridge University Press, 2001).

2. Richard Mckeon, *The Basic Works of Aristotle*, Reprint (Random House, 1941).

3. Ibid.

4. Atul Gawande, *The Checklist Manifesto: How to Get Things Right* (Profile Books, 2011).

5. Ibid.

6. Samuel Moyn, *The Last Utopia: Human Rights in History*, Reprint (Belknap Press, 2012).

7. Martin Heidegger began his career with a phenomenological interpretation of Aristotle, with a particular focus on Book VI of *The Nicomachean Ethics*, which is where Aristotle outlines his ideas on practical wisdom. Martin Heidegger, *Being and Time*, Reprint (Harper Perennial, 2008).

8. Senge, *The Fifth Discipline*.

9. Nassim Nicholas Taleb, *The Black Swan: The Impact of the Highly Improbable* (Penguin, 2008).

10. Alain Badiou, *Being and Event* (Continuum, 2011).

11. http://www.lacan.com/essays/?page_id=323.

12. Taleb, *The Black Swan*.

13. Taking one celebrated example, Badiou points out, "When Galileo announced the principle of inertia, he was still separated from the truth of the new physics by all the chance encounters that are named in subjects such as Descartes or Newton. How could he, with the names he fabricated and displaced (because they were at hand—'movement,' 'equal proportion,' etc.), have supposed the veracity of his principle for the situation to-come that was the establishment of modern science; that is, the supplementation of his situation with the indiscernible and unfinishable part that one has to name 'rational physics'?"

14. David A. Schmaltz, "Unlearning Project Management," http://www.projectsatwork.com/content/Articles/241381.cfm.

15. Nassim Nicholas Taleb, *Antifragile: Things That Gain from Disorder* (Allen Lane, 2012).

Chapter 7

1. Paul Romer first came up with this idea. See Naam, *The Infinite Resource*, 119.
2. Deborah Ancona and Henrik Bresman, *X-Teams: How to Build Teams That Lead, Innovate and Succeed* (Harvard Business Review Press, 2007).
3. Ibid.
4. Ibid.
5. Ibid.
6. C. Wright Mills, *The Power Elite* (Oxford University Press, USA, 2000).
7. Michel Foucault, *Discipline and Punish: The Birth of the Prison* (Random House, 1977).
8. Joseph S. Nye Jr, *Bound to Lead: The Changing Nature of American Power* (Basic Books, 1991); Joseph S. Nye Jr, *Soft Power: The Means to Success in World Politics* (PublicAffairs, 2005).
9. http://blog.quotabl.es/2011/03/16/sxswi-with-bruce-sterling/.
10. Duncan J. Watts and Steven H. Strogatz, "Collective Dynamics of 'Small-World' Networks," *Nature* 393, no. 6684 (1998): 440–42.
11. Duncan J. Watts, *Six Degrees: The Science of a Connected Age* (W.W. Norton & Company, 2004).
12. He writes, "This focus on 'influentials' is mostly based on a view of how we want the world to look versus how it actually works. The network in which word of mouth spreads, including all the people, interactions and communication channels, is generally unobservable because it is so complex. In addition, when we try and understand it, we only look at messages that did spread, and can't observe the ones that did not. This complexity has led us to confuse coincidence and correlation with causality. We look back after an event has occurred, see the most visible person, and assume they have wielded the greatest influence. This is the problem with Gladwell's Law of the Few. It's easier to attribute success to an inspirational person, rather than try and understand the complex network in which they are situated." Paul Adams, *Grouped: How Small Groups of Friends Are the Key to Influence on the Social Web* (New Riders, 2011).
13. Ibid.
14. Ibid.

15. Richard Rumelt, *Good Strategy Bad Strategy: The Difference and Why It Matters* (Crown Business, 2011).

16. Arnold Mindell, *Sitting in the Fire: Large Group Transformation Using Conflict and Diversity* (Lao Tse Press, 1995).

17. Crane W. Stookey, "The Container Principle: Resilience, Chaos, and Trust," *Nova Scotia: The Nova Scotia Sea School* (2003).

18. Steven Johnson, *Where Good Ideas Come From* (Riverhead 2010).

19. Lefebvre, *The Production of Space.*

20. Ibid.

21. Ibid.

Chapter 8

1. http://en.wikipedia.org/wiki/Tactic_(method)#Strategy_versus_tactic.

2. Ken Robinson and Lou Aronica, *The Element: How Finding Your Passion Changes Everything* (Penguin, 2010).

3. Jacques Ellul, *Propaganda: The Formation of Men's Attitudes* (Vintage, 1973).

4. Daniel Coyle, *The Talent Code: Greatness Isn't Born. It's Grown. Here's How* (Bantam, 2009).

5. Seth Godin, *Tribes: We Need You to Lead Us* (Portfolio, 2008).

6. David Robertson and Bill Breen, *Brick by Brick: How Lego Rewrote the Rules of Innovation and Conquered the Global Toy Industry* (Random House Business, 2013).

7. http://hbr.org/2005/07/strategic-intent/ar/1.

8. Thanks to Hans Verolme for the phrase.

Conclusion

1. http://www.theguardian.com/environment/2013/apr/29/global-carbon-dioxide-levels.

2. http://www.pnas.org/content/early/2013/07/26/1312464110.

3. http://stephenschneider.stanford.edu/Publications/PDF_Papers/Schneider-lane.pdf.

4. http://www.theguardian.com/environment/2013/jan/27/nicholas-stern-climate-change-davos.

5. Kevin Kelly, *Out of Control: The New Biology of Machines, Social Systems, and the Economic World* (Basic Books, 1995).

6. Cosma Shalizi, "In Soviet Union, Optimization Problem Solves You" (Paper presented at the the Red Plenty Book Event, 2012).

BIBLIOGRAPHY

Adams, Paul. *Grouped: How Small Groups of Friends Are the Key to Influence on the Social Web* (Voices That Matter). New Riders, 2011.

Ancona, Deborah, and Henrik Bresman. *X-Teams: How to Build Teams That Lead, Innovate and Succeed.* Harvard Business Review Press, 2007.

Badiou, Alain. *Being and Event.* New ed. Continuum, 2011.

Banerjee, Abhijit, and Esther Duflo. *Poor Economics: A Radical Rethinking of the Way to Fight Global Poverty.* Reprint ed. PublicAffairs, 2012.

Barnett, Michael. *Empire of Humanity: A History of Humanitarianism.* Reprint ed. Cornell University Press, 2013.

Bateman, Milford. *Why Doesn't Microfinance Work? The Destructive Rise of Local Neoliberalism.* Zed Books Ltd., 2010.

Bauman, Zygmunt. *Liquid Modernity.* Polity, 2000.

BBC Business News. "Sir Mervyn King: 'Too Big to Fail, Too Big to Jail or Simply Too Big.'" (June 19, 2013).

Beck, Ulrich. *Risk Society: Towards a New Modernity* (Published in Association with Theory, Culture & Society). SAGE Publications Ltd, 1992.

Bevan, Gwyn (LSE), and Christopher Hood (Oxford). "What's Measured Is What Matters: Targets and Gaming in the English Public Health Care System." Discussion Paper Series: No. 0501, 2005.

Bilmes, Linda J. "The Financial Legacy of Iraq and Afghanistan: How Wartime Spending Decisions Will Constrain Future National Security Budgets." HKS Faculty Research Working Paper Series RWP13-006, 2013.

Blumi, Isa. *Chaos in Yemen: Societal Collapse and the New Authoritari-anism* (Routledge Advances in Middle East and Islamic Studies). Reprint ed. Routledge, 2012.

Bonabeau, Albert-László, and Eric Barabási. "Scale-Free Networks." *Scientific American*, 2003.

Bourdieu, Pierre. *The Logic of Practice.* New ed. Polity Press, 1992.

Buffet, Peter. "The Charitable-Industrial Complex." *New York Times*, July 26, 2013.

Butcher, Luke. 2011. Review: The Production of Space. http://luke butcher.blogspot.co.uk/2011/02/review-production-of-space.html.

Cardenal, Juan Pablo, and Heriberto Araujo. *China's Silent Army: The Pioneers, Traders, Fixers and Workers Who Are Remaking the World in Beijing's Image.* Crown, 2013.

Chatham House. 2010. Development Assistance and Humanitarian Aid. www.youtube.com/watch?v=DUHeJYJwd-A.

Clark, Victoria. *Yemen: Dancing on the Heads of Snakes.* Yale University Press, 2010.

Clarke, Richard A., and Robert Knake. *Cyber War: The Next Threat to National Security and What to Do About It.* Reprint ed. Ecco, 2011.

Coyle, Daniel. *The Talent Code: Greatness Isn't Born. It's Grown. Here's How.* Bantam, 2009.

Denning, Steve. The Dumbest Idea in the World: Maximizing Shareholder Value. www.forbes.com/sites/stevedenning/2011/11/28/maximizing-shareholder-value-the-dumbest-idea-in-the-world/.

Diamond, Jared, and James A. Robinson. *Natural Experiments of History.* Reprint ed. Harvard University Press, 2011.

Drezner, Daniel W. *Theories of International Politics and Zombies.* Princeton University Press, 2011.

Ellul, Jacques. *Propaganda: The Formation of Men's Attitudes.* Vintage, 1973.

Flyvbjerg, Bent. *Making Social Science Matter.* Cambridge University Press, 2001.

Flyvbjerg, Bent. *Rationality and Power: Democracy in Practice* (Morality and Society Series). University of Chicago Press, 1998.

Foucault, Michel. *Discipline and Punish: The Birth of the Prison.* Random House, 1977.

Gawande, Atul. *The Checklist Manifesto: How to Get Things Right.* Profile Books, 2011.

Gillham, Patrick F., Bob Edwards, and John A. Noakes. "Strategic Incapacitation and the Policing of Occupy Wall Street Protests in New York City, 2011." *Policing and Society: An International Journal of Research and Policy* Vol. 23, No. 1, 2012.

Godin, Seth. *Tribes: We Need You to Lead Us*. Portfolio, 2008.

Gonzalez, Roberto J. *American Counterinsurgency: Human Science and the Human Terrain*. Prickly Paradigm Press, 2009.

Greer, John Michael. 2005. How Civilizations Fall: A Theory of Catabolic Collapse. www.ecoshock.org/transcripts/greer_on_collapse .pdf.

Hassan, Zaid. "Connecting to Source." *The Systems Thinker* Vol. 17, No. 7, 2006.

Hassan, Zaid. "Slouching Towards Flatlands." *What's the Real Story? Generating a Dialogue around the MDGs*, 2008.

Heidegger, Martin. *Being and Time*. Reprint ed. Harper Perennial, 2008.

Heifetz, Ronald A., Marty Linsky, and Alexander Grashow. *The Practice of Adaptive Leadership: Tools and Tactics for Changing Your Organization and the World*. Harvard Business Press, 2009.

Hoff, Benjamin. *The Tao of Pooh (the Wisdom of Pooh)*. New edition. Methuen Winnie the Pooh, 1998.

Hwang, Victor W. *The Rainforest: The Secret to Building the Next Silicon Valley*. Regenwald, 2012.

Hyde, Lewis. *Common as Air: Revolution, Art, and Ownership*. Farrar, Straus and Giroux, 2010.

Jaworski, Joseph. *Source: The Inner Path of Knowledge Creation* (BK Business). Berrett-Koehler Publishers, 2012.

Jaworski, Joseph, and C. Otto Scharmer. "Leading in the Digital Economy: Sensing and Seizing Emerging Opportunities," 2000.

Johnsen, Gregory D. *The Last Refuge: Yemen, Al-Qaeda, and the Battle for Arabia*. Oneworld Publications, 2013.

Johnson, Steven. *Where Good Ideas Come From*. Riverhead, 2010.

Kahane, Adam. *Power and Love: A Theory and Practice of Social Change*. Berrett-Koehler Publishers, 2010.

Kahane, Adam. *Transformative Scenario Planning: Working Together to Change the Future*. Berrett-Koehler Publishers, 2012.

Kapoor, Ilan. *Celebrity Humanitarianism: The Ideology of Global Charity* (Interventions). Routledge, 2012.

Kelly, Kevin. *Out of Control: The New Biology of Machines, Social Systems, and the Economic World*. Reprint ed. Basic Books, 1995.

Knuth, Marianne. "Kago Ya Bana: Three Years of Working for Children in Midvaal." Paper presented at the Kago Ya Bana, 2010.

Lefebvre, Henri. *The Production of Space*. Wiley-Blackwell, 1991.

Levy, Steven. *In the Plex: How Google Thinks, Works, and Shapes Our Lives*. Simon & Schuster, 2011.

Lewis, Michael. *Moneyball*. W. W. Norton & Company, 2011.

Mckeon, Richard. *The Basic Works of Aristotle*. Reprint. Random House, 1941.

Meadows, Donella H., Jorgen Randers, and Dennis L. Meadows. *The Limits to Growth: The 30-Year Update*. Revised edition. Routledge, 2004.

Mills, C. Wright. *The Power Elite*. Oxford University Press, USA, 2000.

Mindell, Arnold. *Sitting in the Fire: Large Group Transformation Using Conflict and Diversity*. Lao Tse Press, 1995.

Mintzberg, Henry. *The Rise and Fall of Strategic Planning*. Financial Times Prentice Hall, 2000.

Mitchell, Melanie. *Complexity: A Guided Tour*. Oxford University Press, USA, 2009.

Moyn, Samuel. *The Last Utopia: Human Rights in History*. Reprint. Belknap Press, 2012.

Munk, Nina. *The Idealist: Jeffrey Sachs and the Quest to End Poverty*. Doubleday, 2013.

Myatt, Tony, and Rod Hill. *The Economics Anti-Textbook: A Critical Thinker's Guide to Microeconomics*. Zed Books, 2010.

Naam, Ramez. *The Infinite Resource: The Power of Ideas on a Finite Planet*. University Press of New England, 2013.

Naim, Moises. *End of Power: From Boardrooms to Battlefields and Churches to States, Why Being in Charge Isn't What It Used to Be*. Basic Books, 2013.

Nye, Joseph S., Jr. *Bound to Lead: The Changing Nature of American Power*. Basic Books, 1991.

Nye, Joseph S., Jr. *Soft Power: The Means to Success in World Politics*. PublicAffairs, 2005.

Pallotta, Dan. 2013. The Way We Think about Charity Is Dead Wrong. www.ted.com/talks/dan_pallotta_the_way_we_think_about _charity _is_dead_wrong.html.

Phillips, Sarah. *Yemen and the Politics of Permanent Crisis* (Adelphi Series). Routledge, 2011.

"The Politics of Evidence Conference Report." Paper presented at the Politics of Evidence Conference, 2013.

Polman, Linda. *War Games: The Story of Aid and War in Modern Times.* Viking, 2011.

Price, David H. *Weaponizing Anthropology: Social Science in Service of the Militarized State* (Counterpunch). Reprint. AK Press, 2011.

Quiggin, John. *Zombie Economics: How Dead Ideas Still Walk Among Us* Reprint. Princeton University Press, 2012.

Rautenberg, Tom. "Private Memo to Vision Team, Gang of Five, and Surita Sandosham." 2006.

Ray, Deepak K., Nathaniel D. Mueller, Paul C. West, and Jonathan A. Foley. "Yield Trends Are Insufficient to Double Global Crop Production by 2050." *PLOS ONE.* June 19, 2013.

Reeler, Doug. "A Theory of Social Change and Implications for Practice, Planning, Monitoring and Evaluation." 2007.

Rittel, Horst W.J., and Melvin M. Webber. "Dilemmas in a General Theory of Planning." *Policy Sciences 4* (1973): 155–69.

Robertson, David, and Bill Breen. *Brick by Brick: How Lego Rewrote the Rules of Innovation and Conquered the Global Toy Industry.* Random House Business, 2013.

Robinson, Ken, and Lou Aronica. *The Element: How Finding Your Passion Changes Everything.* Penguin, 2010.

Rumelt, Richard. *Good Strategy Bad Strategy: The Difference and Why It Matters.* Crown Business, 2011.

Sandis, Constantine, and Nassim Taleb. *Ethics and Asymmetry: Skin in the Game as a Required Heuristic for Acting Under Uncertainty.* www.fooledbyrandomness.com/SandisTaleb.pdf.

Scharmer, C. Otto. *Theory U: Leading from the Future as It Emerges.* Berrett-Koehler Publishers, 2009.

Schmaltz, David. *The Blind Men and the Elephant: Mastering Project Work.* Berrett-Koehler Publishers, 2003.

Schmaltz, David A. Unlearning Project Management. 2008. www.projectsatwork.com/content/Articles/241381.cfm.

Scott, James C. *Domination and the Arts of Resistance: Hidden Transcripts.* Yale University Press, 1992.

Scott, James C. *Seeing Like a State: How Certain Schemes to Improve the*

Human Condition Have Failed (Institution for Social and Policy
Studies at Yale University). Yale University Press, 1999.

Senge, Peter M. *The Fifth Discipline: The Art and Practice of the Learning
Organization*. Revised. Doubleday, 2006.

Sengupta, Joyeeta, and Vrinda Datta. *Evaluation Reports of the
Maharashtra Change Lab Process*. Mumbai: Tata Institute of Social
Sciences, 2006.

Shalizi, Cosma. "In Soviet Union, Optimization Problem Solves *You*."
Paper presented at the Red Plenty Book Event, 2012.

Shilts, Randy. *And the Band Played On: Politics, People, and the AIDS
Epidemic, 20th-Anniversary Edition*. Revised. St. Martin's Griffin,
2007.

Silver, Nate. *The Signal and the Noise: The Art and Science of Prediction*.
Allen Lane, 2012.

Silver, Nate. *The Signal and the Noise: Why So Many Predictions Fail—
But Some Don't*. Penguin Press HC, 2012.

Simpson, Emile. *War from the Ground Up: Twenty-First Century Combat
as Politics*. C Hurst & Co Publishers Ltd, 2012.

Sorkin, Andrew Ross. *Too Big to Fail: The Inside Story of How Wall Street
and Washington Fought to Save the Financial System—and Themselves*.
Penguin Books, 2011.

Spufford, Francis. *Red Plenty*. Faber and Faber, 2011.

Steffan, Alex. 2005. Winning the Great Wager. www.worldchanging
.com/archives/002197.html.

Stookey, Crane W. "The Container Principle: Resilience, Chaos, and
Trust." *Nova Scotia: The Nova Scotia Sea School*, 2003.

Sweitzer, Susan. "Learning History—Chapter 1." Paper presented at
the Sustainable Food Laboratory, 2004.

Sweitzer, Susan. "Learning History—Chapter 3." Paper presented at
the Sustainable Food Laboratory, 2005.

Sweitzer, Susan. "Learning History—Chapter 4." Paper presented at
the Sustainable Food Laboratory, 2005.

Taleb, Nassim Nicholas. *Antifragile: Things That Gain from Disorder*.
Allen Lane, 2012.

Taleb, Nassim Nicholas. *The Black Swan: The Impact of the Highly
Improbable*. Re-issue. Penguin, 2008.

Tsing, Anna Lowenhaupt. *Friction: An Ethnography of Global Connection*. Princeton University Press, 2004.

UNICEF. 2012. Significant Improvement in Nutrition Status for Maharashtra's Children Under-Two. www.unicef.org/india/Nutrition_Maharashtra.docx

Vis, Jan Kees, Hal Hamilton, and Eric Lowitt. "Chapter Four: Renewing the Global Food System." In *The Collaboration Economy: How to Meet Business, Social, and Environmental Needs and Gain Competitive Advantage*, 256. Jossey-Bass, 2013.

Watts, Duncan J. *Six Degrees: The Science of a Connected Age*. Reprint. W.W. Norton & Company, 2004.

Watts, Duncan J., and Steven H. Strogatz, "Collective Dynamics of 'Small-World' Networks." *Nature* 393, no. 6684 (1998): 440–42.

Wedel, Janine R. *Shadow Elite: How the World's New Power Brokers Undermine Democracy, Government, and the Free Market*. Basic Books, 2009.

Weiss, Thomas G. *Humanitarian Business*. Polity Press, 2013.

Wolfe, Tom. *The Right Stuff*. Picador, 2008.

Worth, Robert. "Is Yemen the Next Afghanistan?" *NY Times Magazine*, 2010.

Zadek, Simon. *The Civil Corporation: The New Economy of Corporate Citizenship*. Earthscan Ltd, 2001.

INDEX

ABOUT THE AUTHOR

Zaid Hassan is the cofounder of Reos Partners, where he currently serves as Managing Partner of the Oxford office. Reos Partners is a social innovation consultancy that addresses complex, high-stakes challenges around the world.

Zaid was born in 1973 in London. When he was seven years old, his parents decided to pack up and move the family, including his twin sister and younger sister, to India. The original plan was to go for two years and get a little experience of the wider world. Instead, they were gone twelve years, traveling the world, moving to Bombay, then to New Delhi, and then finally to the emirate of Abu Dhabi, in the United Arab Emirates.

Zaid came back to the UK in 1992, where he studied physics as an undergrad for a little while (spending most of his time in the lab messing around the with pre-web Internet). His familiarity with the Internet, IP protocols, and rudimentary HTML skills sucked him out of the physics department into the dot-com boom. He worked for a number of years as a freelancer, eventually setting up his own production company, Anthropic, for a few years before working for a NASDAQ listed dot-com. He ended his tech career as Chief Actualisation Officer for a nonprofit tech start-up.

These experiences led him to the State of the World Forum in San Francisco in 1999. Here Zaid connected with hundreds of activists, social entrepreneurs, ambitious start-ups, world leaders, and young people all dedicated to tackling society's most challenging problems. A year later, he found himself working as part of a small global team for a peer-learning youth group called Pioneers of Change. During his two years at Pioneers, he helped run learning programs in countries as diverse as Brazil, India, Egypt, and Mexico, focused on creating systemic change. This marked the beginning of over a decade and a half of experimentation in running social labs.

In 2007 Zaid cofounded Reos Partners.

He rides a single-speed (non-fixie) Genesis bike the color of a sunset.

Zaid currently lives in Oxford with his wife, Mia, and young son, Ashar, who wants to know why we ask questions.

He tweets @zaidhassan.

Reos

Reos is a social enterprise that helps businesses, governments, and civil society organisations address complex social challenges.

We support diverse teams to work together on their toughest problems, through convening, designing, and facilitating strategic responses.

These responses often take the form of agile, action-orientated, multi-stakeholder partnerships and initiatives aimed at changing systems.

Reos brings together a broad range of skills to support these partnerships.

We have extensive experience in a range of domains, including education, health, employment, food, energy, the environment, security, and peace building.

We work both locally and globally at multiple scales.

Our offices are located in Cambridge (Massachusetts), Johannesburg, Melbourne, Oxford, San Francisco, São Paulo, Sydney, and The Hague.

To learn more about us:

Visit our website: www.reospartners.com

Follow us on Twitter: @reospartners

Bursting with practical ideas...

The Social Labs Fieldbook

Menka Sanghvi, Zaid Hassan & Contributors

This is a practical and interactive e-book that will guide you in creating and sustaining an effective social lab with passion, precision, and purpose. It is packed with insights and experience from leading practitioners in the field.

Inside you will find exercises, checklists, examples, and tips. These prompts will help you navigate the many layers of a social lab, from designing group processes, fundraising, stakeholder mapping, agile project management, and governance to rapid prototyping to test your initiatives within its real context.

Who is this book for?

Anyone interested in creating lasting, systemic, solutions to the challenges they face , from government departments, civil society, and community-based groups, to social enterprises, corporations, and, of course, independent change agents.

Available online: www.social-labs.org or on Kindle.
Price US $4.99
Print on demand also available.

Berrett–Koehler
Publishers

Berrett-Koehler is an independent publisher dedicated to an ambitious mission: *Creating a World That Works for All*.

We believe that to truly create a better world, action is needed at all levels—individual, organizational, and societal. At the individual level, our publications help people align their lives with their values and with their aspirations for a better world. At the organizational level, our publications promote progressive leadership and management practices, socially responsible approaches to business, and humane and effective organizations. At the societal level, our publications advance social and economic justice, shared prosperity, sustainability, and new solutions to national and global issues.

A major theme of our publications is "Opening Up New Space." Berrett-Koehler titles challenge conventional thinking, introduce new ideas, and foster positive change. Their common quest is changing the underlying beliefs, mindsets, institutions, and structures that keep generating the same cycles of problems, no matter who our leaders are or what improvement programs we adopt.

We strive to practice what we preach—to operate our publishing company in line with the ideas in our books. At the core of our approach is stewardship, which we define as a deep sense of responsibility to administer the company for the benefit of all of our "stakeholder" groups: authors, customers, employees, investors, service providers, and the communities and environment around us.

We are grateful to the thousands of readers, authors, and other friends of the company who consider themselves to be part of the "BK Community." We hope that you, too, will join us in our mission.

A BK Business Book

This book is part of our BK Business series. BK Business titles pioneer new and progressive leadership and management practices in all types of public, private, and nonprofit organizations. They promote socially responsible approaches to business, innovative organizational change methods, and more humane and effective organizations.

Berrett–Koehler
Publishers

A community dedicated to creating
a world that works for all

Dear Reader,

Thank you for picking up this book and joining our worldwide community of Berrett-Koehler readers. We share ideas that bring positive change into people's lives, organizations, and society.

To welcome you, we'd like to offer you a free e-book. You can pick from among twelve of our bestselling books by entering the promotional code **BKP92E** here: http://www.bkconnection.com/welcome.

When you claim your free e-book, we'll also send you a copy of our e-newsletter, the *BK Communiqué*. Although you're free to unsubscribe, there are many benefits to sticking around. In every issue of our newsletter you'll find

- A free e-book
- Tips from famous authors
- Discounts on spotlight titles
- Hilarious insider publishing news
- A chance to win a prize for answering a riddle

Best of all, our readers tell us, "Your newsletter is the only one I actually read." So claim your gift today, and please stay in touch!

Sincerely,

Charlotte Ashlock
Steward of the BK Website

Questions? Comments? Contact me at bkcommunity@bkpub.com.

MIX
From responsible
sources
FSC® C113845

Certified

Corporation
bcorporation.net